Learning
Communication Theories

A Student Guide for Theories of Human Communication

Seventh Edition

Stephen W. Littlejohn
University of New Mexico

WADSWORTH
THOMSON LEARNING™
Australia • Canada • Mexico • Singapore • Spain • United Kingdom • United States

Printed in Canada.
1 2 3 4 5 6 7 05 04 03 02 01

0-534-54958-6

For more information about our products, contact us at:
Thomson Learning Academic Resource Center
1-800-423-0563

For permission to use material from this text, contact us by:
Phone: 1-800-730-2214
Fax: 1-800-731-2215
Web: www.thomsonrights.com

Asia
Thomson Learning
60 Albert Complex, #15-01
Albert Complex
Singapore 189969

Australia
Nelson Thomson Learning
102 Dodds Street
South Street
South Melbourne, Victoria 3205
Australia

Canada
Nelson Thomson Learning
1120 Birchmount Road
Toronto, Ontario M1K 5G4
Canada

Europe/Middle East/South Africa
Thomson Learning
Berkshire House
168-173 High Holborn
London WC1 V7AA
United Kingdom

Latin America
Thomson Learning
Seneca, 53
Colonia Polanco
11560 Mexico D.F.
Mexico

Spain
Paraninfo Thomson Learning
Calle/Magallanes, 25
28015 Madrid, Spain

Contents

WELCOME TO COMMUNICATION THEORY

You are about to embark on a challenging and exciting experience shared with thousands of other students in communication programs throughout the United States and abroad. Communication theory may sound imposing, difficult, and dry, but it can be one of the most exciting courses you will take.

I have written this workbook to help make the course clear, interesting, and useful. The workbook is a companion to *Theories of Human Communication.* Your instructor and the text will provide the basic information, and this workbook will provide a variety of tools to help you understand and apply it. I know that students are individuals and have various needs, so I have tried to include a variety of material in this book to be interesting and helpful to the many types of students who will use it. You will like some parts better than others, and within the constraints of your particular course, you should feel free to use those parts that suit your needs and skip other sections.

I once had a student who said, "The trouble with communication theory is that it is too theoretical." Actually, theory is inherently practical, and you can become a better communicator if you have a knowledge of theory. You really can't do anything without theories to guide you. Theories give you ideas about what is important, why it is important, what to do, and how to do it. How do therapists know how to help people? Theories tell them. How do filmmakers, television directors, and music producers know how to create and sell their products? Theories tell them. How do business managers know how to organize? Theories tell them.

People learn theories from school and from personal experience. They don't always know they are using theories, but they are. Virtually everything you learn in school is related to theory in one way or another. How, then, do teachers know what to teach? Theories tell them.

Take a television production course as an example. Here you learn how to construct a program, how to set a stage, use lights, operate cameras, write, edit, and a host of other skills. All of these aspects of production are guided by theory, and different producers operate differently because they have different theories of what makes a good television program.

All of your courses have theories in them. The communication theory course pulls much of this material together so that you can see what makes a theory and the different approaches to theories. If you think of the course as nothing more than a list of theories to memorize, it will be dreadful. But if you think of it as a set of useful ideas, and you are willing to apply those ideas to your life, this course will be both useful and satisfying. Your instructor should provide some guidance on how to do this, and this workbook will include lots of ideas and insights for learning and applying the material.

Many students think that there must be one right theory of communication, so they wonder why the course has so many theories. Imagine trying to coach a football team with only one play. The team would be severely crippled because it would have no options and it would not be able to figure out what the other team is doing. If you only have one way of understanding how relationships work, you can look forward to a rocky road to romance. If you see organizations and businesses in only one way, you can look forward to long waits in the unemployment line.

Communication theory is practical, but it is important for another reason as well. A college education, as opposed to vocational training, does not just teach you how to do things. You will learn techniques and methods on your own and in various training programs throughout your life. In college, most everything you do provides cognitive insight or ways of thinking. A college curriculum presents a series of idea games, puzzles, and problems to work out. Students who come to love ideas and learn to enjoy playing with them love school. Students who see ideas as obstacles merely endure it.

Our culture tends to labor under the weight of an unfortunate value—that everything we do must lead to something else. Nothing has value unless it builds a bridge, makes some money, wins a lover, or sells a product. Yet the happiest, most well adjusted and productive members of society love life for its own sake. They seek out experiences just to have them. They love ideas. Colleges and universities accomplish much in society, but one of their most important functions is that they expose vast segments of our population to the value of ideas.

One of my best friends has been a university professor, a leader in his church, an expert whitewater guide, an amateur archaeologist, a writer, a champion bridge player, a hobby woodworker, and a world traveler. He has always been open to new experiences, and he learned early in life to be open to ideas and the pleasures of the mind. This kind of mental adventure can begin in courses like communication theory.

Communication theory is an idea game. Learn to enjoy playing with theories just as you enjoy playing music, sports, games, and other pleasures of life. What good is a chess game? Why would anyone want to chase a little ball around a three-mile course? Why would someone spend hours wading through a mystery novel?

Why sew a dress when your closet is full of clothes? Why spend an afternoon in the kitchen creating a new recipe when you could just plop a frozen meal in the microwave? And why spend months studying a foreign language that you will use only occasionally? People do these things because they enhance life. Ideas are just as intrinsically valuable as any other way in which we occupy our minds.

So you can begin communication theory with one of two attitudes. You can either have fun with it and use it as a way to develop your mind, or you can dread and endure it and miss an opportunity for self-development. I am saddened by the college graduate who misses the most important opportunity the baccalaureate provided—the pleasure of ideas.

What Communication Theory Can Do For You

I indicated above that communication theory can be useful. Here is a list of some specific ways:

1. It provides a wealth of ideas that can be used in other classes. Once you know several communication theories, you will never run out of ideas for projects and papers in other classes. You will have theories that can be used in a variety of communication courses to help analyze cases and experiences and add to discussion in class. Most professors love to see you make insightful connections in their classes.

2. It provides excellent preparation for graduate school. If you are planning to go to graduate school or if you are already enrolled in such a program, communication theory provides excellent background for many of the subjects you will study. Many students who have had communication theory say that it helped them immeasurably in their graduate studies.

3. It provides ways to analyze and understand difficult communication problems in your life. The first step to overcoming communication problems is to have a way to understand what is going on. Theories provide insights into problems. They tell you what to look for, how people might respond, and even some ways to deal with difficulties.

4. It suggests areas for further development and training. In this class you will learn aspects of communication that appeal to you and areas that do not. You will discover new interests and ideas for other classes to take.

5. It provides tools that can be used on the job. You will learn about how people interact, how they solve problems in groups, how organizations operate, some problems in media, how people think, and a host of other practical concerns.

6. It provides an opportunity to sharpen your critical thinking skills. By understanding, relating, analyzing, and criticizing theories of communication, you will further develop some general skills that will serve you well in all aspects of life.

7. It can provide insights that will make you a better communicator. By understanding various ways in which people respond in interpersonal, group, organizational, and mass communication, you will be able to adapt to audiences, adjust messages to situations, and gauge effects as you communicate with others in a variety of settings.

8. It shows you how to solve conceptual problems. It helps you figure things out. Throughout life you will encounter strange and difficult situations that demand your attention and analysis. Often you will have to think through new situations in new ways. All communication theories have been created for the purpose of explaining and understanding events in new ways. By studying the process of theory construction, you will develop the ability to create your own theories.

Suggestions for Learning Communication Theory

Communication theory may be one of your most difficult classes. You can make it easier on yourself by following some simple guidelines.

First, keep a positive attitude. Consider the course as a challenge and have fun with it. Use the course to prove to yourself that you can really accomplish something important. Keep an open mind. Don't get bogged down looking for the correct solution or the right theory. Consider theories to be suggestions or options about how to think about communication. Look for theories that you think are most useful or interesting from your perspective. Consider the course to be a cafeteria of ideas. Avoid unnecessary discouragement. You will encounter some difficult ideas in this course, but you must not get discouraged if you don't understand them at first. In time, understanding will occur.

Second, maintain perspective. Don't get stuck in needless detail. Your first response to the book or the lecture may be that there is too much material. Find out from your instructor just how much of this detail is important. Approach it with perspective and look for the big picture before concentrating on minor points. Don't become overly concerned with memorization. Although your instructor may require some memorization, the most important objectives of the course deal with understanding, analysis, application, and critique. This is the fun stuff. Devote a considerable amount of your study time to these higher-order learning objectives. Work with and think about the ideas in the theories, apply them to your experiences, and make use of the workbook to develop your thinking skills.

Third, make use of the resources available to you. Make good use of the instructor, teaching assistants, tutors, and other students. Know your instructor's office hours, don't be afraid to ask questions, and find an appropriate support system. Study groups can work very well in this course, and if you need more personal attention, talk to your instructor about working with a more advanced student.

Fourth, manage your time. Don't procrastinate. You will double or triple the difficulty of the course if you delay reading and other assignments. Some students procrastinate because they are afraid of the material. This pattern is ironic because procrastination gives you something to really be afraid of, Get right to work, read regularly and steadily, and begin papers and projects as soon as they are assigned. Spread out the reading. The chapters in the book are long and contain quite a bit of information. You don't have to read an entire chapter all at once. If you try to do so, you will probably become discouraged.

Memory Work

Regardless of the approach taken by your instructor, some memory work will be required. Some instructors require more than others. One of the keys to being a good student is learning to put memorization in perspective. If you concentrate on it as if it were the most important part of being a student, you will find your education to be a drag. If you realize that it is a step toward something bigger and more important and you concentrate on other objectives in addition to memorization, the course and your entire college experience will be more satisfying.

First, realize that your instructor will probably not require you to memorize the entire book. There will probably be some selectivity, and you need to find out as accurately as possible what kinds of things the instructor wants you to know. This gives you an idea of what to study. This is not the same thing as knowing *what is* going to be on the test. Rather, it means knowing *what kind of information* is considered important.

Once this is established, you can concentrate on learning the materials. Here are some practical ideas to make the job easier:

1. Make use of the outline in the workbook as a guide to the material and important concepts.

2. Work the glossary-building exercises in each chapter of the workbook.

3. Use mnemonic devices. These are games or tricks that students use to make associations with the information. Mnemonic devices make memory work more fun and a lot easier. For example, you can turn a list of items into a clever phrase that is easy to remember. For example, there are nine functions of theory: (O)rganizing, (F)ocus, (C)larifying, (O)bservation, (P)redictive, (H)euristic, (C)ommunicative, (C)ontrol, and (G)enerative. Make a cute sentence out of this: 'One out of four cats obtains pet hats and coats from the cat god.' Memorize the sentence, and you will easily remember the nine points.

4. Use the examples in the book to help you learn the information. Think about the example and apply the theory's concepts to it. As you recall the examples, you will also recall the concepts. This technique is especially important because it focuses on application and understanding. It is also a lot more interesting than memorizing an abstract list.

For example, Chapter Seven discusses post-decisional dissonance, which is the tendency to change your mind after making a big decision. You can easily remember this by thinking about the example presented in the book of the study of people who had recently bought a car. Fewer customers who were called after signing the contract to be reassured changed their mind than those who were not called. If you remember this example, you remember what post-decisional dissonance is and you remember an important communication principle as well.

How to Use This Study Guide

The chapters of this study guide correspond to the chapters of the book. Each chapter has seven sections:

1. A chapter map
2. A word puzzle
3. Internet challenges
4. Using your whole brain
5. Theory to action
6. Cases
7. Critical incidents

The chapter maps should help you get a sense of the relationship among the concepts in the chapter, and they will be an excellent checklist for your studying. More than this, however, you should play with these maps. Try mapping the chapter yourself. Use different graphics. Try it by hand or by computer. Each time you grapple with the relationship among concepts, you will be learning important new dimensions of the material.

The next part of each chapter is a word puzzle. Once again, these exercises are intended to be challenging, but interesting, and they serve to help you learn the chapter in an intriguing way.

Next are the Internet and whole brain challenges. You will find that these exercises give you an opportunity to play with the ideas and to apply them. The case analyses and critical incidents show you how the theories can be applied to actual situations.

Your instructor will provide guidelines on how to use the workbook. Some instructors may require you to complete certain exercises or case analyses. How you use the book will depend on the approach taken by your instructor and your own learning style.

I suggest that you go back and forth between the text and workbook. For example, you will probably want to read the introduction and glance at the outline before skimming the chapter in the book for the first time. After a careful reading of the chapter, you may want to look more carefully at the chapter map to solidify your understanding of the material. If you have trouble with the word puzzles, you may want to go back to the chapter to check on some definitions and then try the puzzle again. Don't worry if you have to look things up as you go. That is just part of the learning process.

No matter how you decide to use this workbook, I am confident that if you take it seriously, you will learn the course material very well indeed.

Communication Theory and Scholarship

Theory in the Process

System Theory

Theories of Signs and

Theories of Discourse

Theories of Message I

Theories of Message I

Theories of Symbolic

Theories of Social and

Theories of Experienc

Critical Theories

Communication in Relationships

Communication in Group Decision Making

Communication in Organizational Networks

Communication and Media

Chapter 1

Communication Theory and Scholarship

- What is theory and where does it come from?
- What distinguishes communication theory as a field?
- How do people generate knowledge?
- What are the types of communication theory?
- How is the field organized?

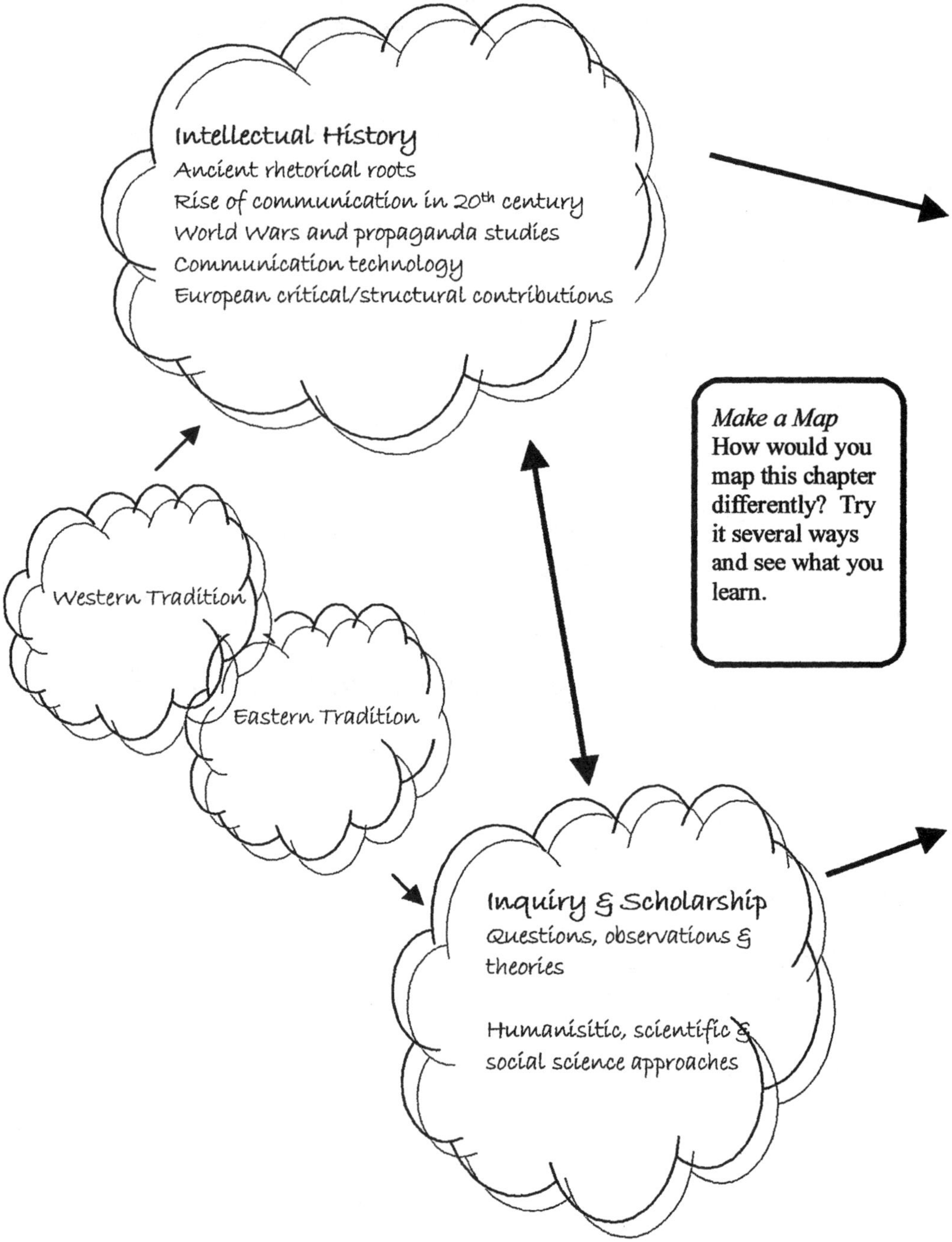

Make a Map
How would you map this chapter differently? Try it several ways and see what you learn.

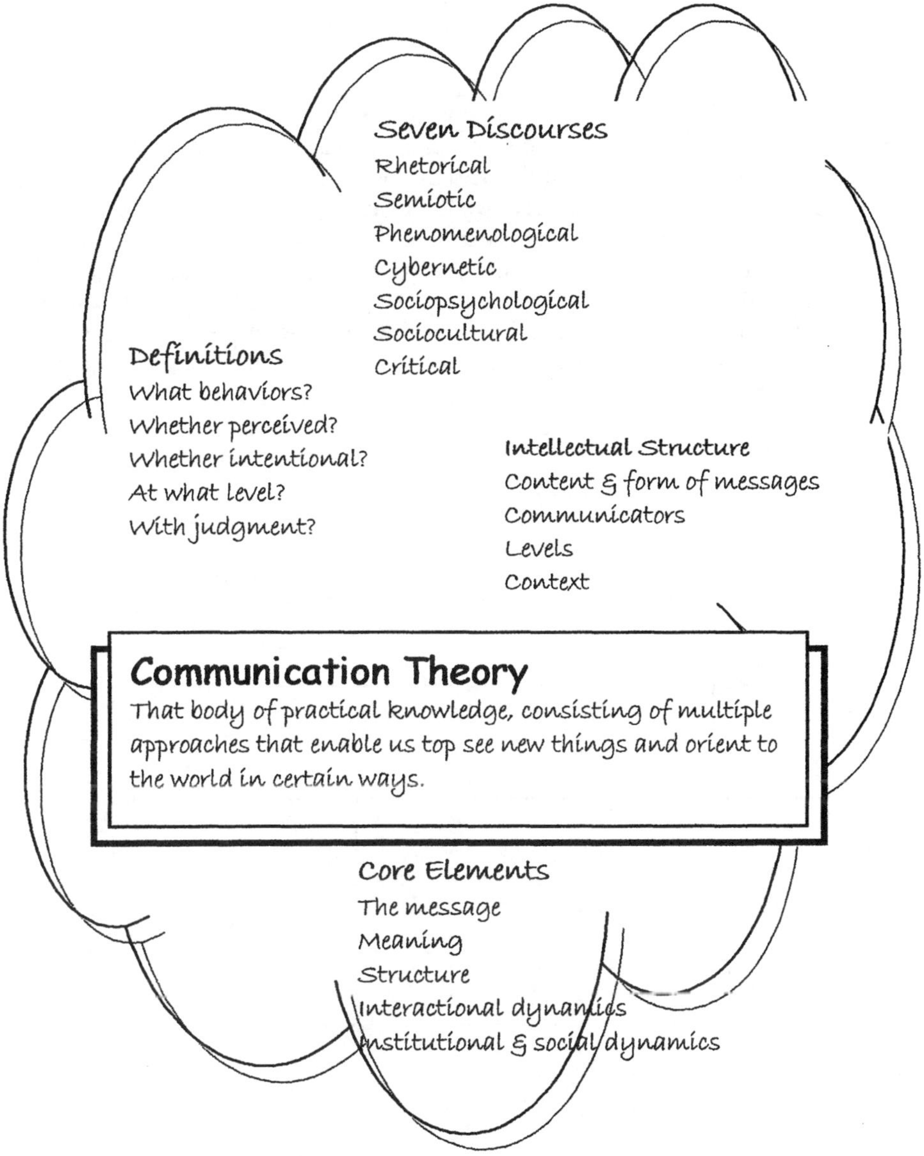

Chapter 1 Map
Communication Theory and Scholarship

WORD PUZZLE

Your objective is to build the pyramid by writing the correct term in each building block. Work down the list of definitions on the opposite page in order from 1-10, writing words in each block as you go. Begin with the bottom row, left to right, and move up one layer when you finish the row. You cannot move to the next block until you write a term in the previous block. If you know the correct word, write it on the block; then move on. If you must look the word up in the book, write "looked up" in the space next to the definition. When you are finished with all 10 words, check the pyramid on the back of the next page. Each word that you knew without looking it up is worth 2 points. Each correct word you had to look up is worth 1 point. Each incorrect term is worth 0. Count up your total score when you are finished.

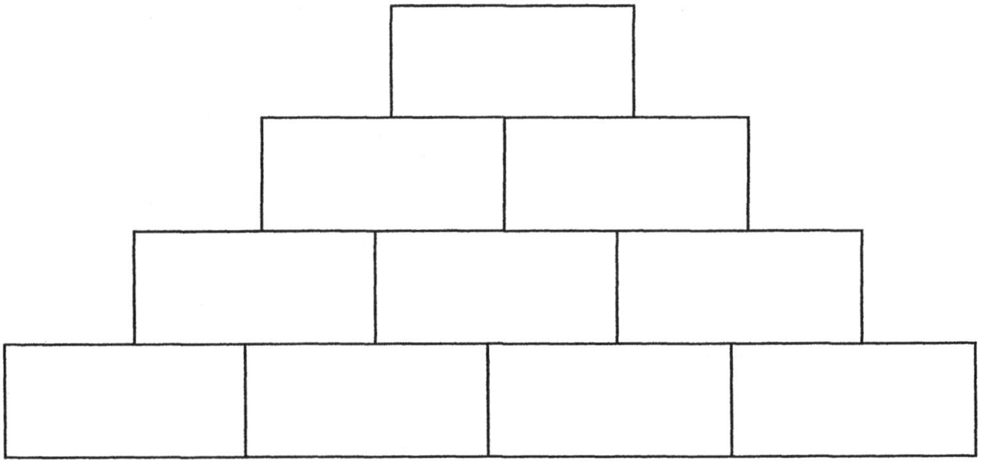

Definitions:

1. Any attempt to explain or represent an experience.
2. A statement of success or accuracy in a definition.
3. The systematic study of experience that leads to understanding and knowledge.
4. Aesthetic, pragmatic, and ethical qualities of the observed.
5. The branch of knowledge that attempts to look at the world in such a way that all observers, trained the same way and using the same methods, would see the same thing.
6. The tradition that honors a vocabulary of senders and receivers, information, feedback, redundancy, and systems.
7. Public communication, usually mediated.
8. The type of communication theory that focuses on general concepts and processes common to all communication.
9. The part of the world in which intuitive insight gained from experience is most honored.
10. The branch of scholarship that focuses on subjectivity.

Answer:

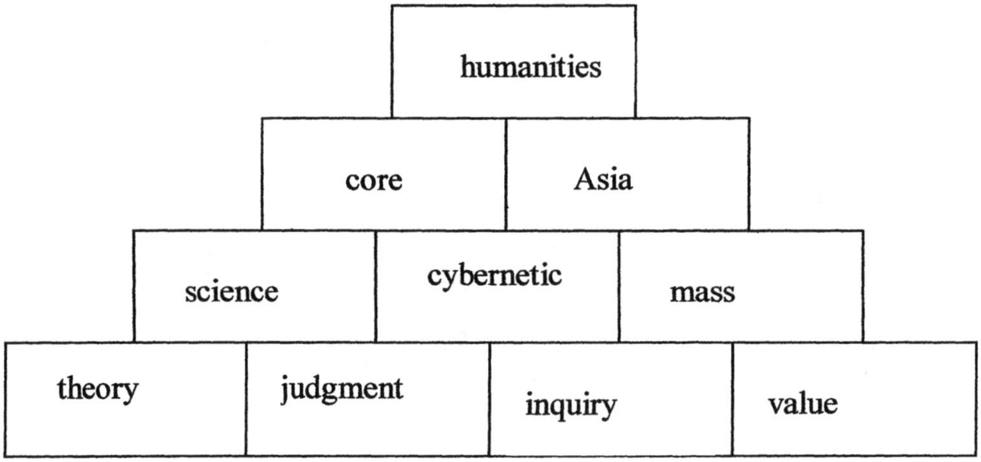

humanities
core
Asia
science
cybernetic
mass
theory
judgment
inquiry
value

CHALLENGES

Internet Challenges

1. *Speed Search*: Set a timer for 10 minutes. Find as many definitions of communication as you can in this period of time. Mark each page with a bookmark and put these in a folder for future reference.

2. *Communication Theory*: Search for sites on "Communication Theory," and see what you come up with. Look for several sites and compare these. To broaden your search, think of key terms other than "communication theory."

3. *College Mission Statements*: Identify five colleges and universities of different types (e.g., religious, liberal arts, small and large, graduate research institutions, state and private, etc.) Go to their websites and see if you can find a mission statement. How do these statements vary, and to what extent to they reflect the types of scholarship discussed in this chapter?

Using Your Whole Brain

Thumb through the chapter and write important terms and phrases on an unlined piece of paper. Do not make a list, but write these terms freeform using different styles and angles. Get as many terms on the page as you can, and aim for a "look" that pleases you. Now move to your computer. Transfer your word collage to the computer, manipulating even more variables. You may wish to use Microsoft's Word Art feature, but any program you like will do. Keep playing with the piece until you are pleased with the result. You may want to print it and keep it with your class notes.

THEORY TO ACTION

Assign members of a small group to play the role of scientist, humanities scholar, and social scientist. Have a discussion of the following topics within your respective roles. After the discussion, debrief the experience and explore the ways in which science, humanities, and social science shapes the views and styles of group members. Which of these roles were most and least comfortable for you and why? Which roles seem most suited to which topics and why?

Topics:

- Genetic engineering
- Medical ethics
- Science and religion
- Personality
- Community building
- Race relations
- Education
- Great authors and artists
- Wildlife management
- Environmental issues

CASES

My Case: Graduation Requirements from a College Catalogue:*

To satisfy general education requirements, students must complete a minimum of 36 semester units distributed in five areas as described below. The general education program is designed to achieve certain broad goals so students become educated persons in three ways: by developing the ability to think and communicate clearly and effectively; by acquiring knowledge about the arts, humanities, science, and society; and by understanding the methods, principles and processes of human inquiry.

To meet the objectives, courses comprising the general education program enable the student to explore the perspectives, methods of inquiry, assumptions, fundamental knowledge and values of various disciplines. This exploration prepares the student to perceive the relationships between the disciplines in preparation for a lifelong commitment to scholarship and learning.

Area A: Oral and written communications, critical thinking (9 units)

The courses in area A sharpen a student's ability to think clearly and logically, to find and critically examine information, and to communicate orally and in writing. The courses in written and oral communication and the course in critical thinking help a student when he/she takes other courses at the university.

Area B: Physical universe, life forms, and mathematics (9 units)

General education in the natural sciences and mathematics focuses on the physical universe and its life forms. This requirement helps students cope with and participate in the changing world. The program objectives, recognizing the importance of scientific methods as investigative tools, present science as a unified discipline with a major impact on the human condition.

Area C: Arts, literature, philosophy, and humanities (9 units)

Arts/humanities courses seek the cultivation of imagination, sensibility and sensitivity in the cognitive, physical, and emotional aspects of human experience. Students are encouraged to respond subjectively to experience and to develop discrimination as to the integrity of the emotional response.

Area D: Human social, political, and economic institutions and behaviors and their historical background (9 units)

Area D courses introduce students to the scholarly study of human experience, emphasizing one or more of the following concepts: culture; ethnicity; place; time; the economy; the political community; behavioral, emotional and, cognitive processes; and human interaction and organization.

*Excerpts adapted from the Humboldt State University catalogue.

My Analysis: This case is a description from a college catalog of a portion of a university's graduation requirements. Upon close reading, it appears that this program is designed to do two general things: to promote good communication and critical thinking skills and to help students understand the process of inquiry in the three major branches of knowledge—the sciences, the humanities, and the social sciences.

The communication portion of this curriculum makes certain assumptions about what communication is. This definition seems to be low in *level of observation* because it relates primarily to writing and speaking. It is *intentional* in orientation because it envisions writing and speaking as something people do to accomplish goals, and it is *normative* because it implies that some communication is better than others and that students can learn how to be better communicators.

The other portions of the curriculum seem to be related quite directly to science, humanities, and social science as described in Chapter 1 of our text. Science makes use of the scientific method to discover the nature of the physical universe. The courses chosen for this area of general education are apparently chosen for this purpose. The description of the humanities and arts courses, however, is quite different. These seem to stress not the outside world, but the person and his or her subjective and emotional response. Here we see an example of the major distinctions made in this chapter.

The description of social science in this case is less clear about the approach to be taken, but it does emphasize human concerns such as politics, economy, history, geography, psychology, anthropology, etc. If Chapter 1 of our text is accurate, the courses in this area of the curriculum would emphasize many of the issues addressed in the text discussion of social science. The various genres of theory would probably be encountered in the social science segment. For example, cognitive and behavioral approaches would probably be encountered in the psychology course; the structural and functional approaches would probably be encountered in the sociology course; the interpretive approach might be found in the anthropology course; and the critical approach might be encountered in the political science or the sociology course.

In sum, this general education program seems to be designed with the goal to help students understand what knowledge is and how it is created. The science portion would emphasize discovery, the humanities and arts portion interpretation and criticism, and social sciences some blend of both. What these areas probably share in common is the basic model of inquiry described in Chapter 1—asking questions, making observations, and drafting answers. The forms that this model takes in each area, however, differ substantially from one another.

Your Case: Read the general graduation requirements in your own college or university catalog and analyze them in terms of the concepts from this chapter.

CRITICAL INCIDENT

Explaining Your Major

Over the winter break, you attend a family holiday party. Your favorite uncle, a nuclear physicist at Livermore National Laboratories, approaches you at the party and asks how school is coming along. This uncle has always taken a keen interest in your life and wants to see you succeed almost as much as your parents do. So you take his question quite seriously.

Not quite knowing what response to expect, you answer tentatively, "Okay, I guess."

"Just okay?" he asks rather sternly. "What did you say your major is?" Although you have told him previously, he has forgotten.

"Communication," you answer. There is a pause while your uncle scrutinizes you.

"What is that, exactly?" It is clear that he hasn't a clue.

Your answer is important because you want your uncle to respect your choices and to realize that you have chosen a good major. You want him to have confidence that you will have a good career in a meaningful field. He is a scientist, and you suspect that he really does not understand much about the communication field. For him communication means the internal wiring of a computer or satellite communication. You know, too, that your uncle is truly interested and will listen if you give him a chance.

So what will you say in answer to his question?

Communication Theory and Scholarship

Theory in the Proce

System Theory

Theories of Signs a

Theories of Discou

Theories of Messag

Theories of Messag

Theories of Symbo

Theories of Social a

Theories of Experience and Interpretation

Critical Theories

Communication in Relationships

Communication in Group Decision Making

Communication in Organizational Networks

Communication and Media

Chapter 2

Theory in the Process of Inquiry

- **What do theories do?**
- **What does a theory look like?**
- **What are different ways of thinking about theories?**
- **How are theories evaluated?**
- **How are theories different from one another?**

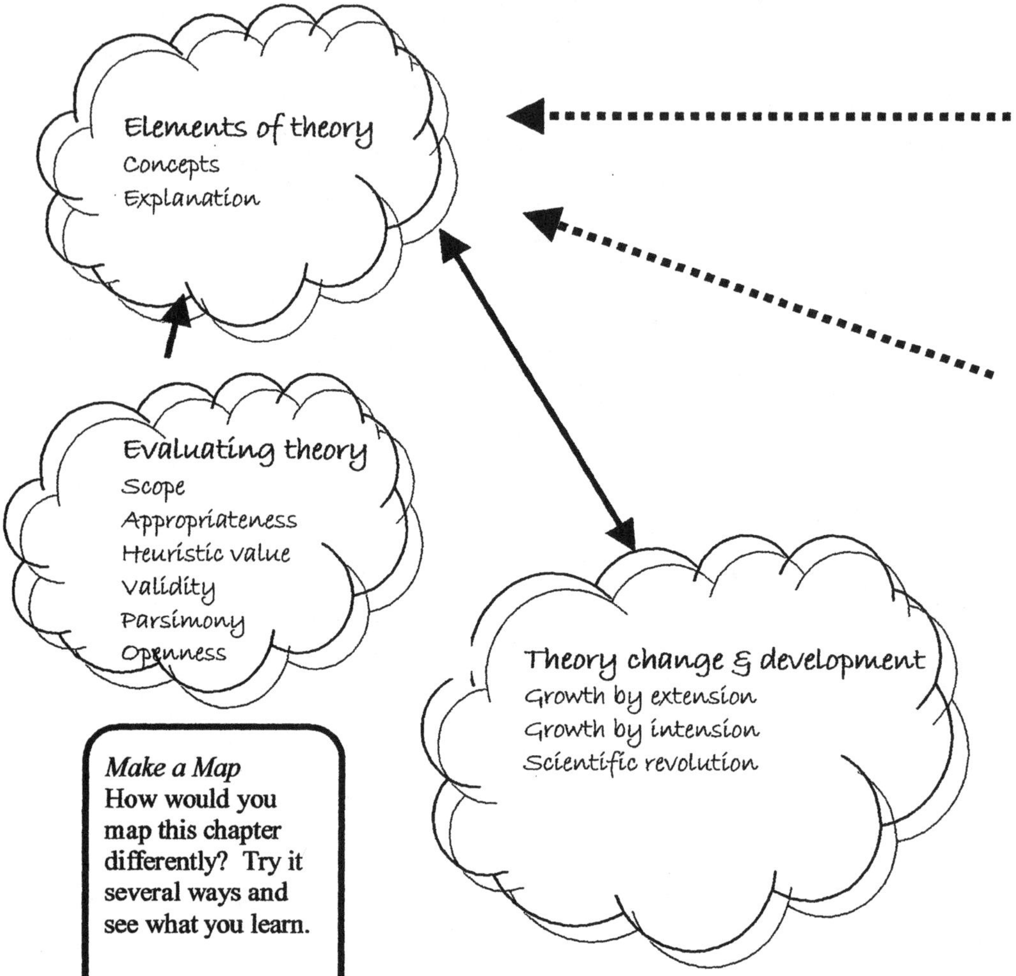

Make a Map
How would you map this chapter differently? Try it several ways and see what you learn.

Chapter 2 Map
Theory in the Process of Inquiry

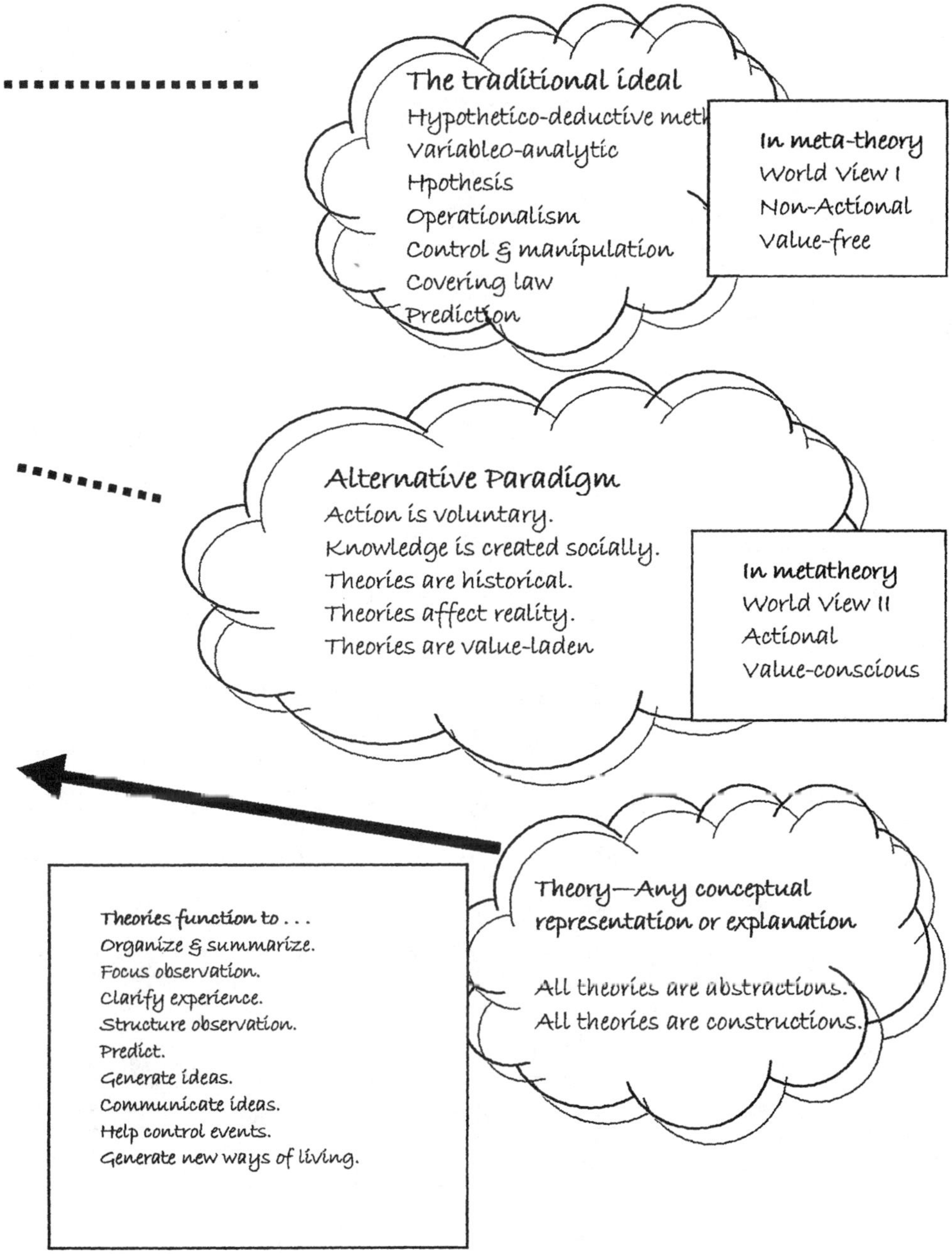
The traditional ideal
Hypothetico-deductive meth
Variableo-analytic
Hpothesis
Operationalism
Control & manipulation
Covering law
Prediction
In meta-theory
World View I
Non-Actional
Value-free
Alternative Paradigm
Action is voluntary.
Knowledge is created socially.
Theories are historical.
Theories affect reality.
Theories are value-laden
In metatheory
World View II
Actional
Value-conscious
Theory—Any conceptual representation or explanation
All theories are abstractions.
All theories are constructions.
Theories function to . . .
Organize & summarize.
Focus observation.
Clarify experience.
Structure observation.
Predict.
Generate ideas.
Communicate ideas.
Help control events.
Generate new ways of living.

WORD PUZZLE

There are 17 words or word combinations from this chapter in the grid below. Circle as many as you can find—across, down, and diagonal.

I	S	M	E	T	A	T	H	E	O	R	Y	B	H	X	Z	O	T
C	A	U	S	A	L	E	X	P	L	A	N	A	T	I	O	N	R
E	O	T	Z	B	I	H	R	M	N	F	G	A	T	I	O	R	U
P	A	R	S	I	M	O	N	Y	O	A	C	L	N	Q	T	A	C
I	R	S	H	L	Z	G	B	T	A	X	O	N	O	M	Y	T	T
S	H	E	P	Y	O	O	S	D	G	I	N	I	V	U	P	I	L
T	O	T	D	S	P	O	G	B	D	O	C	L	F	R	W	O	G
E	L	S	T	I	S	O	R	G	H	L	E	M	R	O	A	N	V
M	P	L	G	D	C	O	T	T	R	O	P	V	E	W	A	A	A
O	P	U	L	A	T	T	E	H	V	G	T	B	A	D	K	L	L
L	A	W	Y	E	R	A	I	O	E	Y	Z	T	L	B	C	I	I
O	S	S	O	L	A	T	E	O	T	S	V	W	I	D	G	S	D
G	O	T	S	O	M	E	T	I	N	S	I	T	S	G	D	M	I
Y	S	O	P	E	R	A	T	I	O	N	I	S	M	V	T	K	T
A	W	E	S	O	M	E	R	E	L	I	A	B	I	L	I	T	Y

NOTES

Answer:

I	S	M	E	T	A	T	H	E	O	R	Y	B	H	X	Z	O	T
C	A	U	S	A	L	E	X	P	L	A	N	A	T	I	O	N	R
E	O	T	Z	B	I	H	R	M	N	F	G	A	T	I	O	R	U
P	A	R	S	I	M	O	N	Y	O	A	C	L	N	Q	T	A	C
I	R	S	H	L	Z	G	B	T	A	X	O	N	O	M	Y	T	T
S	H	E	P	Y	O	O	S	D	G	I	N	I	V	U	P	I	L
T	O	T	D	S	P	O	G	B	D	O	C	L	F	R	W	O	G
E	L	S	T	I	S	O	R	G	H	L	E	M	R	O	A	N	V
M	P	L	G	D	C	O	T	T	R	O	P	V	E	W	A	A	A
O	P	U	L	A	T	T	E	H	V	G	T	B	A	D	K	L	L
L	A	W	Y	E	R	A	I	O	E	Y	Z	T	L	B	C	I	I
O	S	S	O	L	A	T	E	O	T	S	V	W	I	D	G	S	D
G	O	T	S	O	M	E	T	I	N	S	I	T	S	G	D	M	I
Y	S	O	P	E	R	A	T	I	O	N	I	S	M	V	T	K	T
A	W	E	S	O	M	E	R	E	L	I	A	B	I	L	I	T	Y

CHALLENGES

Internet Challenges

1. *Strange Words*: Identify several words in Chapter 2 that are new to you. These will probably be philosophical or technical terms. Using several search engines, see if you can find any hits on these terms. Now think of more ordinary synonyms for these technical terms, and use these key words in your search. What insights do you gain from this activity.

2. *Authors*: Several authors are referenced in this chapter. See if any of websites. What do you learn about them from their sites?

3. *Finding Theories*: Select a topic in which you have an interest. Find some websites on this topic. Look closely at what is said about the topic at these sites. What implicit theories are used in these descriptions and explanations. How would you classify these theories based on the metatheoretical categories discussed in this chapter?

Using Your Whole Brain

Select an art medium of your choice. You might consider pastel, charcoal, pencil, or clay. (Children's modeling clay would be great.) Without thinking about it, let your imagination guide you in creating abstract depictions of the following contrasting concepts:

Worldview I ~ Worldview II

Actional Theory ~ Non-actional Theory

Value-free scholarship ~ Value-conscious scholarship

THEORY TO ACTION

Identify two faculty members you would like to know better. Ask them what their favorite theories are and why. Have a discussion with each about their favorite theories in terms of the concepts from this chapter.

CASES

My Case: Developing a Theory

Jeremy Sutra had been a teaching professor in a communication department at a California State university for fifteen years and was taking a sabbatical to renew his research skills and begin a concentrated research program. He had decided to visit another university to work with a group of well-known researchers. After making the necessary contacts, he had been accepted and welcomed as a visiting professor in a major communication program in Massachusetts.

Soon after arriving in the northeast, he began working with Josh Winters, a highly published and well-respected scholar in the communication field, on a study of the conflict between the Moral Majority and its liberal critics. The study involved the careful examination of the discourse, including speeches, newsletter articles, books, tapes, and films, produced by each side in this conflict. Jeremy and Josh worked throughout the year on a paper on this problem to be submitted for publication.

In the meantime, Josh had been approached by the university's mediation center about studying the dispute mediation process. The mediation center specialized in helping citizens settle their disputes of all kinds through negotiation and compromise. Josh asked Jeremy if he would like to participate, and Jeremy agreed enthusiastically. Over the course of several months, they and a group of students videotaped and observed a number of mediation sessions, some successful and others not. They also interviewed the mediators to find out what they thought of the sessions. Jeremy wrote up a report of the cases they had observed and later presented it at a convention.

It did not take long for Josh and Jeremy to realize that the Moral Majority and mediation studies had much in common. Both had to do with conflict and interaction between people with different ideas about the world. Certain mediation sessions seemed very much like the interactions they had observed between the Moral Majority and its critics, including the fact that they seemed intractable and did not get settled. The researchers began to explore some reasons why these types of conflicts; were so hard to settle and hypothesized that the opponents had such different views of the world that they had no common method for evaluating one another's arguments or making a decision as to which side was right. They made a commitment to look into this problem in more detail.

Soon after Jeremy returned to California, he began to study the case of the gay and lesbian rights movement in the church. He saw this as an opportunity to gain additional insights into the problem of difficult, irresolvable conflicts. After interviewing several people involved in this conflict and examining the documents they had produced, he and some of his students wrote papers that were later presented at conventions. Jeremy had become so interested in this problem that he decided to take a semester's leave from his university and return to Massachusetts to continue working on it with Josh.

When Jeremy arrived in the northeast, he found Josh busily working on a newly developed dispute intervention program at the university. This program was designed to help people understand and possibly solve the kinds of difficult conflicts in which Jeremy and Josh had become interested. The program had sponsored public symposia on such topics as U.S. involvement in Nicaragua, animal rights, gay and lesbian rights, and CIA recruiting on campus. Jeremy immediately plunged in, became involved in the program's committee, and sat in on a number of conflict sessions sponsored by the new program.

During this second stay in Massachusetts, Jeremy continued working on mediation and with a graduate student conducted a detailed study of a divorce mediation that shared many of the characteristics of the other conflicts Josh and Jeremy had studied. During this period, they decided to codify what they had learned about conflict and write a paper on it.

They had come to call this kind of situation "moral conflict" because it seemed to involve deep differences in beliefs about right and wrong. They found that in moral conflicts, the "moral orders," or belief systems, of the disputants were "incommensurate," which means logically incompatible, and that their differences were therefore far deeper and more philosophical than the surface disagreement might suggest.

They also found that such conflicts often result in inept forms of discourse like shouting matches and slogans, which they came to call "reciprocated diatribe." They hypothesized that diatribe is a result of frustration caused by neither side understanding the other, and they felt that moral conflict was persistent and irresolvable because of the lack of a common set of standards for evaluating arguments. They found, however, that this type of harsh interaction could be overcome if parties were willing to share their deeper assumptions about reality in what they called "transcendent eloquence."

Now, several years later, these researchers have done more case studies and are writing a book about their theory of moral conflict.

My Analysis: This case illustrates several aspects of the development of theory. It shows how theories arise as answers to questions about things that scholars observe. Josh had become interested in the Moral Majority and found that the conflict between this organization and outsiders was not only difficult, but shared features with other conflicts. Even personal conflicts such as those found in mediation can share these characteristics. So he and his colleagues set out to try to explain this type -of conflict.

The resulting theory has a number of concepts, such as moral conflict, moral orders, incommensurate realities, reciprocated diatribe, and transcendent eloquence. Both causal and practical necessity were used in the theory's explanation. Moral conflicts were viewed as caused by the clash of incommensurate moral orders, and the course of the conflict itself was seen as the outcome of communicators' attempts to achieve their goals. Thus the theory involved both empowered and enabling explanations which were primarily person-centered.

The work of Jeremy and Josh is not traditional social science. It did not make use of the hypothetico-deductive method nor did it seek universal covering laws. Because of the use of case studies and interpretation rather than control, manipulation, and measurement, the research program was more in the "alternative paradigm" tradition. As such this work is probably more in the World view II camp than World view 1. It is definitely actional in orientation because it looks at the ways in which people try to accomplish their own objectives in conflict and the consequences of their actions. It is also value-conscious because it is sensitive to the harms of conflict and seeks to find ways to mitigate the damaging effects of moral conflicts.

The Sutra-Winters theory serves several functions. First, it helps the researchers organize and summarize what they have observed about moral conflicts. Second, it helps to focus their attention on particular important aspects of conflicts in their case studies. Third, it clarifies what happens in certain kinds of conflicts, and, fourth, it gives the researchers ideas about interesting events to examine. Fifth, the theory helps them to tell other people what they have done and observed, and sixth, it suggests solutions to be pursued.

The theory is probably a fairly good one. It does not cover a very broad domain, but it does explain a large number of events encountered in everyday life. Some would say that the theory is appropriate and consistent with the kind of events being studied and that more traditional social science methods would not have been very useful with this kind of problem. The theory seems to have heuristic value because it stimulates an unending potential of case studies. It also seems to have some validity in that it has pragmatic value, corresponds with observations made of real events, and seems to be generalizable to a number of cases. Finally, the theory is parsimonious, relying on a few very rich concepts.

Your Case: Student Research Project*

Suzanne Brown was a Speech Communication major taking her first communication theory course. Each student in the class was required to do a research project in order to pass the course. Since she had to choose her subject early in the semester, Suzanne decided to pick a subject that was of personal interest to her, empathy. The professor teaching the course asserted that empathy was something experienced only at the physical level-like getting sick when you see someone else throwing up - not a cognitive experience at all.

Suzanne disagreed with this view of empathy and decided to do research to find out just what the theorists in the field had said about it. What's more she wanted to find out if other people besides herself had the kinds of experiences she called empathy. Thus, in addition to doing a review of literature Suzanne prepared a survey and asked members of a class to respond to her questionnaire.

Suzanne found out in her review of the available literature that the word "empathy" meant different things to different scholars. As a result, she refrained from using that term at all in her questionnaire. Instead, she used the term 'indirect communication." After gathering some demographic data about the respondents, the questionnaire posed questions like, "Have you ever thought you knew what someone else was thinking without their telling you either verbally or nonverbally?' as well as asking the longest distance at which such occurrence took place and how often the subject was "right" about the situation. Other questions asked about the relationship between the subject and the other person, the location and activity of the subject when having this experience, and how it made the subject feel when it happened.

Suzanne had approached this research as an inquiry into the nature of empathy as described by scholars and the experience of empathy (or lack there of) as reflected by responses to her survey. She had thought that her survey would show that women would report more of these indirect communication experiences than men. She was wrong! Her summary stated in part:

> Empathic Communication is not limited to any particular group designated within my categories of sex, age, marital status or parenthood. No apparent profile by sex, age, marital status or parenthood emerged regarding who would have this experience, how often they would have it, or at what level of intensity. Respondents' perceptions of the experience regarding distance, accuracy, and who it happened with seemed to change based on marital status and, to some extent, parenthood.
>
> Survey responses were divided as to whether they were a cognitive or affective experience, which was compatible with the other research cited. The question whether it is all the same process viewed from different perspectives or several look-alike processes remains unanswered.
>
> One only has to use the word "empathy" to create a storm of controversy over what it is that is being studied. The lack of a clear, comprehensive, and widely accepted definition of empathy makes research in this area difficult. As a result, and for use in my own future research, I would like to propose the following definitions:
>
> Affective Empathy. The feelings of another as felt by the empathizer.
>
> Cognitive Empathy. The thought process used by the empathizer to understand and label the feelings experienced via Affective Empathy, and decide what to do about them.
>
> Communicative Empathy. The verbal or nonverbal expression by the empathizer which is a response to the feelings of another and results from a decision to communicate during the Cognitive Empathy process.

Functional Empathy. A system in which Affective, Cognitive, and Communicative Empathy work together to allow each of us to feel, understand, and respond to the legitimate needs and aspirations of others.

Suzanne noted in this first research project that the results of her efforts had provided her with more questions than answers. In subsequent semesters she pursued the subject of empathy in terms of its development in the individual and its use in relationships.

*Adapted from a case study by Roberta Gray.

Your Analysis: Using the concepts in Chapter Two, what method was Suzanne using, was it appropriate to the subject of her research, and what types of results did she present? Explain the theorizing she was doing. How would you approach a similar project? Why?

CRITICAL INCIDENT

The Grant

One of your professors has received a grant to study the communication between environmentalists and the timber industry on the northcoast. The grant includes money for student assistants, and you have been selected to work on the project. The position comes with a very nice stipend, and the experience you will gain by working with the research team is undeniable.

The first job of the team is to decide how to approach the problem—what to study and how to do it. The professor has made it clear that she expects every member of the team to be a creative and active member, so you have a responsibility for making suggestions and being a full participant in all of the discussions. Your professor wisely knows that less experienced researchers such as students often ask excellent questions and make very creative suggestions that more experienced researchers might overlook. She selected you because you did very well in her communication theory course, and she knows you are intelligent and insightful. She also knows that you have a good basic background in inquiry and theory. She is not concerned that you do not know a lot about research methods. Other members of the team will supply that.

You have decided that you want to do a great job from the very beginning, so you are giving the problem considerable thought. You want to come to the first meeting with a well-formed plan of how the group might proceed. Create a plan based on the material from this chapter.

NOTES

Chapter 3

System Theory

- What is a system?
- What are the qualities of systems?
- How do systems govern themselves?
- How do systems use information?
- What does a communication system theory look like?

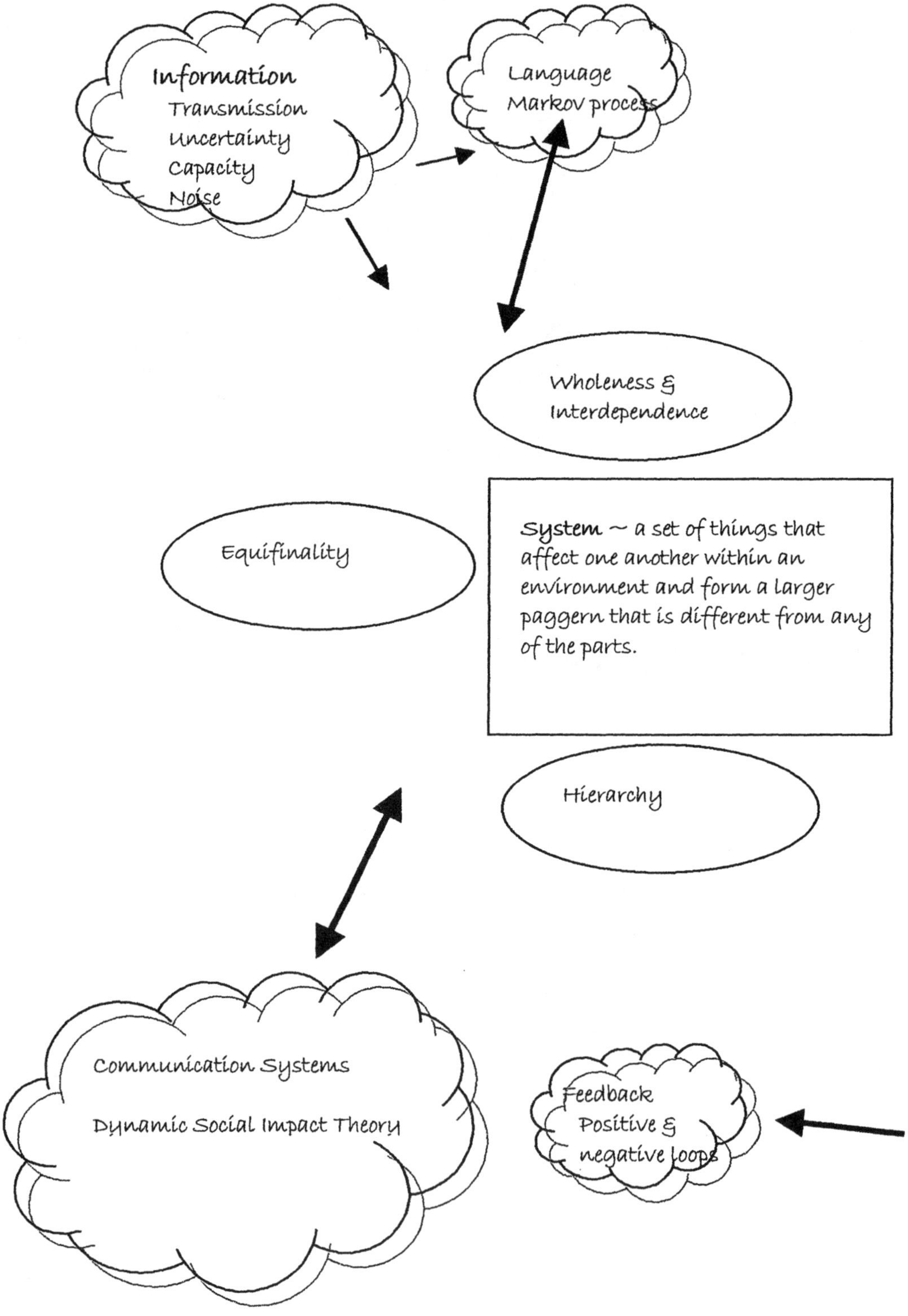
Information
Transmission
Uncertainty
Capacity
Noise
Language
Markov process
Wholeness &
Interdependence
Equifinality
System ~ a set of things that affect one another within an environment and form a larger paggern that is different from any of the parts.
Hierarchy
Communication Systems
Dynamic Social Impact Theory
Feedback
Positive &
negative loops

Make a Map

How would you map this chapter differently? Try it several ways and see what you learn.

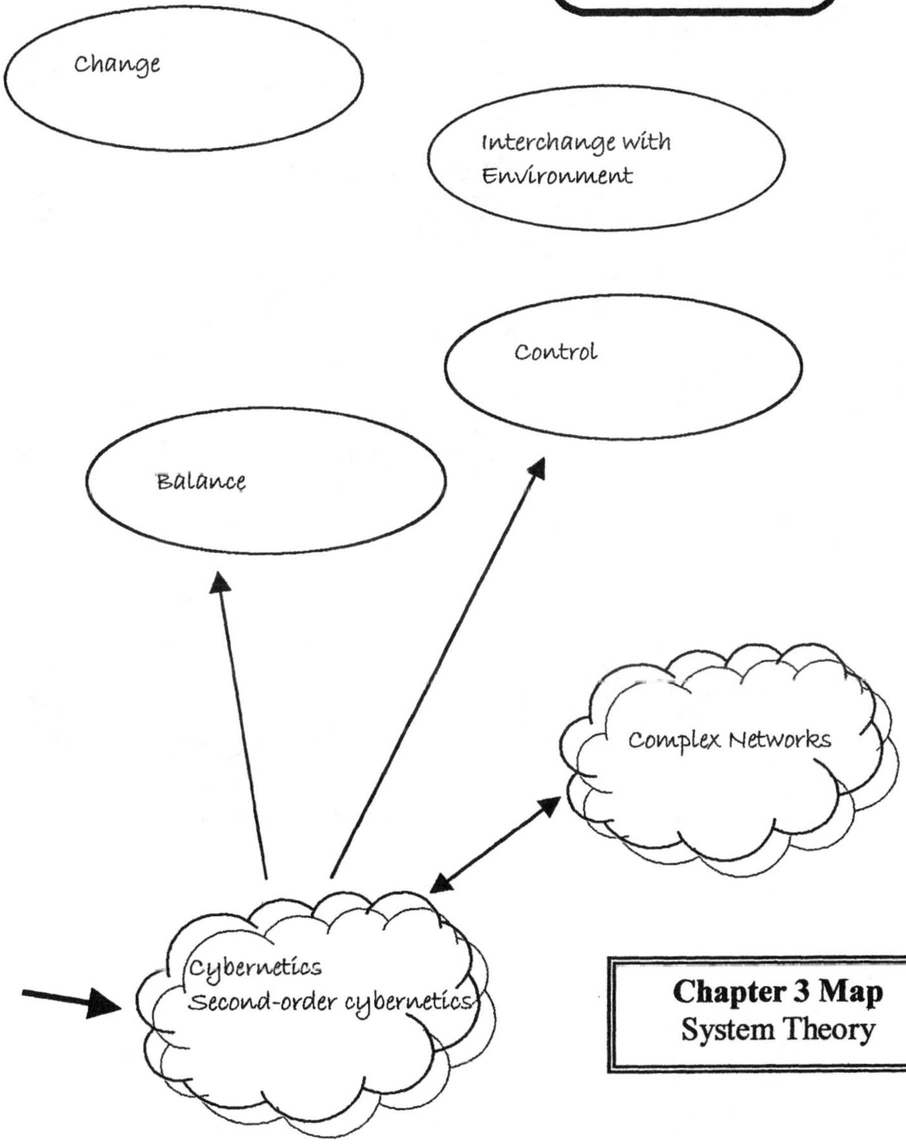

Chapter 3 Map
System Theory

WORD PUZZLE

ACROSS

1. The result of positive feedback
5. Not normally considered a system.
8. A series of complex feedback loops (abb).
12. Sub-sub-sub system.
15. Controlled by a simple cybernetic mechanism.
19. Hierarchy of systems.
25. General Systems (abb).
27. Needed to run a system.
33. What a predictive cybernetic system does.
37. Place where this book was published (abb).
39. A cybernetic system must pay ________ (abb).
43. Common term for "channel capacity."
49. Crucial input for a system that provides mechanical power (abb).
54. ______________ chain.
61. Devices that close off inputs to ocular system.
66. Output of complex cybernetic system common at night (abb).
71. System boundary.
75. Code common in information systems (abb).
77. Wrote *The Knower and the Known*
85. Person doing this puzzle.
88. What systems do as a result of morphogensis
94. What systems need to change.

DOWN

2. ____________ system.
5. Complex biological system.
6. Response to one kind of information in brain.
8. Feedback that counteracts deviation.
9. Possible result of negative feedback.
12. Part of 5 (above).
19. Study of a critical organic subsystem.
21. ___________-order cybernetics.
22. Physical analog of Shannon & Weaver's model.
39. Once used to preserve a zoological system.
47. Element of a system.
51. What system says when it gets negative feedback.
58. The mood of the author when he wrote this puzzle.
64. Huge closed system.
68. End result of closed system.
72. Everyday analogy for steady state.
78. What happens to a closed system.
79. An international system (abb).

ACROSS

1. MORE
5. BOX
8. NET
12. LOW
15. HEAT
19. NESTED
25. GS
27. ENERGY
33. AIM
37. CA
39. ATTN
43. ROOM
49. IGN
54. MARKOV
61. LIDS
66. REM
71. THIN
75. AI
77. GRENE
85. YOU
88. MORPH
94. TIME

DOWN

2. OPEN
5. BOX
6. OW
8. NEGATIVE
9. EASING
12. LEG
19. NEUROLOGY
21. SECOND
22. TRAM
39. ARK
47. PART
51. NO
58. ORNERY
64. SUN
68. MASH
72. HOME
78. ROT
79. EU

CHALLENGES

Internet Challenges

1. *Exploring a Network:* Select a subject that interests you. Get out a pad of paper and pen. Initiate a search, and select a site that has several links to other sites. As you link from one site to the next, construct on the paper the network of sites that you visit. Every time you click a link, note this link on the paper. Make lines between each site and see how the network of sites develops. Continue doing this until the network expands to the point of revealing a system of sites. In what ways is the Internet a system? What does the Internet have in common with other systems, and how is it different from other system?

2. *Cybernetics*: Do a search of "Cybernetics." How many sites come up? Now limit the search by including other key terms such as *feedback, second-order, network, control, system,* and *computer*. Once you have a somewhat limited list of sites, browse through the first several pages of sites and find one or two that look interesting. Check these out.

3. *Dynamic Social Impact Theory*: Search for Dynamic Social Impact Theory. What comes up? Check out several of these sites to see what various people are doing with this theory.

Using Your Whole Brain

As you read through this chapter, begin doodling. You can write in the margins of the text or a separate piece of paper. Let the two sides of your brain work at the same time. When you come to a concept, think about what it means, and let your right brain doodle as you do so.

After you complete this exercise, think about the following questions:

1. Did you have trouble letting both sides of your brain work at the same time? In other words, could you think about a concept while your hand was doodling, or did you need to shift back and forth from thought to doodle?

2. How was your doodling connected to the concepts as you worked through the chapter? Do your doodles in any way reflect the content of the chapter, and if so, how?

3. In what ways did your doodling reflect your mood as you worked through the chapter?

4. Did the doodling exercise cause more stress, or did it relieve stress? Why?

5. Are you a doodler normally, or was this unusual for you? What did you learn about yourself in this exercise?

6. For you, did the doodling enhance your learning or hinder it? Why? Would others find doodling helpful?

THEORY TO ACTION

Identify two systems—a non-human system such as a computer or engine and a human system such as an organization or familiy. For each of these, identify the parts and then look for how the parts relate to one another and affect one another. You can describe the system in words or, if you prefer, a system map or flow chart. (You can find nifty computer programs that will draw flow charts for you.) In mapping the system, be sure to look for wholeness. In other words, how do the parts interact in a way that creates something larger than the sum of the parts?

Now compare the two systems. What are some fundamental differences between human and non-human systems?

CASES

My Case: Campus Life

Helen Lefkowitz Horowitz has written an intriguing history of college life in the United States.* In the early part of the previous century, three types of college students emerged—the college men, the rebels, and the outsiders. Together, these groups came to constitute the culture of undergraduates in our country. Each group has its own way of thinking and acting, and each plays a vital role in college life. These groups have varied over the years in their size and prevalence within colleges and universities.

For the most part, the early norm for campus life was established by the college men. The other groups contrast with this norm in various ways. The college men were a basically conservative group that dominated college life up through the 1950s. These students value group loyalty and collective responsibility above all, which is why they have perpetuated the fraternity system. Between 1920 and 1960 about a fourth to a third of all college students belonged to a Greek society. In the east the proportion was even higher. In their early years, these groups tended to be exclusionist, racist, and sexist. Sexual conquest was an important value to them.

After women began to go to college in larger numbers in the early part of the twentieth century, a female counterpart to the college man developed. These college women found meaning in clubs and sororities, where they learned feminine roles and sought to find a proper husband, usually a college man.

Originally, college men as a culture began in the nineteenth century as a rebellion against the authority of the faculty. College men could not win in a direct struggle against the faculty, so they got power by creating their own culture that was at odds with that of the faculty. These students played the college game, but they did not value it academically. The real learning experience for them occurred in the extracurricular activities of the group. What was learned in the peer group prepared the college men for the world of business, which they felt the humanities and science requirements in the curriculum at that time could not do. College life in this form was at its peak in the first half of this century, up to the 1960s. The ideal of the college man declined in the 1960s, although it has never gone away completely.

The rebels have always opposed the ethic of the college man. Most often rebels took the academic side of college life most seriously. They tended to be individualistic in orientation and opposed the conformity so evident among college men. For the most part, rebels tended to be politically liberal and critical of the kind of society that produces the college men. Over the years, rebels have demanded that colleges deal with the problems of society as a whole. They supported the faculty and curriculum when they felt they could use these to their political advantage, and they rejected them when they perceived that the faculty and curriculum did not serve their needs.

There was much rebel activity in colleges and universities in the early 1900s, up to World War 11. During the 1950s when the country was so security conscious, the college man reigned, and rebel activity subsided. Although college men and rebels always struggled with one another, the rebels came to the fore in the 1960s. During this period the rebels won out as radicalism became synonymous with student rebellion. The 1960s were dramatic, but exaggerated by the media. Actually less than 30% of the students in 1969 participated in any demonstration. During this period the rebels fought against all establishment norms, including the university system and curriculum. This was a shift from earlier times when rebels often used the university system to their advantage. The rebels declined rapidly in the 1970s.

Outsiders have always existed in colleges and universities. The outsiders are the students who really do not belong to either of the other two cultures. In fact, this is probably the majority of students at most points in history. Naturally, the outsiders have little collective identification. They tend to be individualistic and are pursuing their own agendas. Over the years scholars, commuters, veterans, career-oriented students have all been outsiders at one time or another. Even women were outsiders before they began attending in large numbers. College women were not following the typical path for women at that time and seemed odd on the campus. They went essentially ignored by the men and had little to do with them.

Throughout most of the twentieth century, the outsiders have done their own thing alongside the college men and the rebels. They have always been a major part of colleges, but they are less obvious. The 1970s and 1980s were a real period of dominance for outsiders. People actively pursued their own interests during these times. The career-oriented decade of the 1980s was perfect for the outsiders, who experienced considerable stress during this period because of their desire for economic success.

Campus Life: Undergraduate Cultures From the End of the Eighteenth Century to the Present (Chicago: University of Chicago Press, 1987).

My Analysis: This book describes three major subsystems in the overall system of college life. College life itself has changed because these subsystems have changed. Since the college-life system is a hierarchy, we could analyze it on any level. For example, we could consider the college men, the rebels, and the outsiders to be elements of the larger system. As such, these elements can easily be shown to interrelate and affect one another, so that campus life itself is more than the sum of the three groups.

On another level, college life as a suprasystem can be viewed as the environment in which the systems of the college men, the rebels, and the outsiders operate. Here, each group has inputs from and outputs to this environment. They adjust to the environment, and changes occur in each as the overall environment changes. So, for example, whereas women were largely ignored in the nineteenth century when few attended college, as their numbers swelled in the years after the turn of the century, they played an increasingly important role in all three systems.

Both homeostasis and morphogenesis are apparent in the course of college life over the years. Members of each group act in various ways to maintain themselves. The rigidity of the fraternity system, including its racism and sexism, illustrates this balance-achieving work. At the same time, as changes in the environment occurred, morphogensis also came about. For example, rebels up until the 1960s generally supported the faculty and curriculum because they saw these as a way to achieve their political goals. But in the 1960s the rebels rejected the academic system because they saw it as antithetical to their goals. This is an example of moving from a steady state to a growth state. Perhaps the rebels never established a new steady state after this period. One could argue that the student rebellion of the 1960s burned itself out because of its failure to achieve homeostasis.

The 1980s was a period of careerism in college life. Most students during this period pursued their individual career goals with great stability. For these students, most of the inputs were carefully channeled into actions designed to graduate and get a good job. The principle of equifinality is illustrated by these students' ability to use a vast variety of resources in many different ways to meet this goal. If the 1960s was a period of unbridled change, the 1980s was a period of great stability and balance.

Your Case: Planning a Convention

The Western States Communication Association consists of about 1,200 professors and teachers of communication. Every year the association has its convention in February at a city in the western region. The convention planning begins about three years ahead of time when a site is chosen. The Time and Place Committee solicits bids from various university departments willing to sponsor and plan the convention in a hotel near their campus, and these sponsors make presentations to the association's Executive Council. The Executive Council chooses the location based on the attractiveness of the various sites presented. The Executive Secretary then negotiates a deal with a local hotel to put on the event.

The convention is planned by two groups of people. The first is the local arrangements committee, a group from the sponsoring institution, that works with the hotel and makes all of the detailed arrangements, from printing the convention program to ordering and delivering equipment. The second group consists of the President-Elect and a committee of about twenty interest-group chairs. Their responsibility is to plan the program, including the speakers, panels, and events.

The president elect, who will automatically become president the following year, is responsible for overseeing the program planning process. Most of the program consists of presentations and papers by members, who submit their work for review to the interest groups of the organization. Each interest-group chair is responsible for coordinating the review process and recommending programs to the president elect.

The program-planning process begins a year in advance when all the interest group chairs meet to discuss the procedures that will be followed in planning the convention. There are forms, deadlines, and policies about how things are to get done. One of the president elect's most important duties is to keep the interest-group chairs and the local arrangements committee informed of planning developments throughout the year. The program must be completely planned about three months before the convention, so the printed program can be prepared and the membership can be informed about the various events that will take place at the convention.

The association has a particular method for insuring continuity from year to year. Each year the association elects a first vice president. This individual will become the president elect and plan the convention the following year. After that he or she will become president and coordinate the association's business. The first vice presidency is basically a training position. During this year of service, the individual works with and learns from the current president elect.

Your Analysis: Analyze the planning of a convention in terms of system principles. Make use of such concepts as wholeness, interdependence, hierarchy, feedback and control, homeostasis, information and redundancy, Markov chain, convergence, and others. Use other conventions and groups with which you are familiar.

CRITICAL INCIDENT

Housemates

You are a young, single professional in Seattle. You moved there two years ago and have been renting an apartment in a very nice Victorian mansion near downtown. Various parts of the house are all rented to people like yourself, so there is some common interest and a good deal of interaction among the members of this little "community."

The living situation is pleasant. Each person rents two or three rooms. The rooms are spacious and nicely decorated. The rent is pretty high, but you don't have to worry about furniture or utilities, and you can walk or take the bus to work. You are saving a lot of money right now, and the convenience to work and the city is excellent. There is also a spectacular view of Puget Sound from the large bay window in your apartment. You don't see this as a permanent living situation, but is is great for now. Basically, you lucked out.

The tenants share several common areas, including a period-decorated parlour, halls, dining room, and a huge and well-outfitted kitchen. The common areas are available for entertaining on a first-come, first-served basis. A sign-up sheet is kept on a small French-provincial table in the entry way adjacent to the huge double front door. None of the apartments has an exterior entry, so everyone must come in through one of three outside doors and go to their apartment through common spaces. Each tenant has his or her own bathroom, but there are only rudimentary cooking facilities in the apartments, so most of the residents do make use of the kitchen, some more than others. The owner, a widow, drops by a couple times a week to check on things. She is friendly and never seems to object to anything anyone is doing.

Anywhere from six to eight singles live in the house at one time, and you have lived there longest. Several people have come and gone, but four, including yourself, have been in the house over a year. You couldn't help but get to know these people pretty well. You are closest to Sally, who lives across the hall from you. She has become a good friend. You often go out with her to various events in the city. The other two "yearlings' are Bob, an architect, who wishes they could design houses like this now; and Tom, a dentist.

Recently, Sally confided that Tom has been coming on to her, and it is getting a little creepy. He bumps into her around the house at inappropriate times, and he always looks at her in a weird kind of way.

Consequently, she has been spending more time in her room with the door closed. Personally, you like Tom. You're not buddies or anything, but you have never noticed anything strange about him.

You begin to think something is really wrong when Sally abruptly cancels a dinner party she has planned. Thinking she might be ill, you go to her apartment the next morning and knock gently. She tells you through the closed door that she is okay but doesn't want to see anybody. This is certainly her right, but you begin wondering if you have offended her in some way. You decide to stay away.

Later that evening you mention Sally's bizarre behavior to Bob, saying nothing about Tom. Bob says that Tom too has voiced concern about Sally. You decide to leave well enough alone for now.

You don't see Sally for two days, which is really unusual, and when you run into Tom on your way to work, you decide to explore the issue with him. You ask him if he has seen Sally around lately. He says that he has. He tells you that they went out together two nights before. You express surprise and say you didn't realize they were dating. "Oh, we're not," Tom replies, "it was just a test kind of thing. We hit it off real good, though." He says that he thinks Sally is kind of interested in him from the way she has been acting around the house. He says that he told Bob about it, and Bob had encouraged him to ask her out.

You think about this odd situation off and on throughout the day. That evening, you try Sally again. You knock on her door, and she opens it up. She looks good and is friendly. She invites you in. The two of you chat for a few minutes, and then you say, "You know. I've been a little concerned 'cause I haven't seen much of you lately."

"Oh, I've just been real busy," she replies. Nothing about Tom.

In the next few days, Sally seems to be her old self. She leaves her door open and spends more time downstairs. Things must be going pretty well with Sally and Tom, you think. So when you see Tom, you ask him directly: 'How's it going with Sally."

"Oh, I've been gone to a dental convention. Haven't even seen her. By the way, you know Sally pretty well. I think she likes me. Don't you think so?" You just smile, and Tom smiles knowingly back.

Two days later Sally knocks gently on your door and upon entering tells you that she is thinking of moving because of Tom. She says that he has been looking weird again. She says that she really can't afford to move, but she doesn't like the atmosphere. She asks you what you think she should do.

What do you tell her? Take a system perspective in your response.

NOTES

Chapter 4

Theories of Signs and Language

- **What is a sign and how does it work?**
- **How are signs organized?**
- **How is language structured and produced?**
- **How do we use nonverbal signs?**

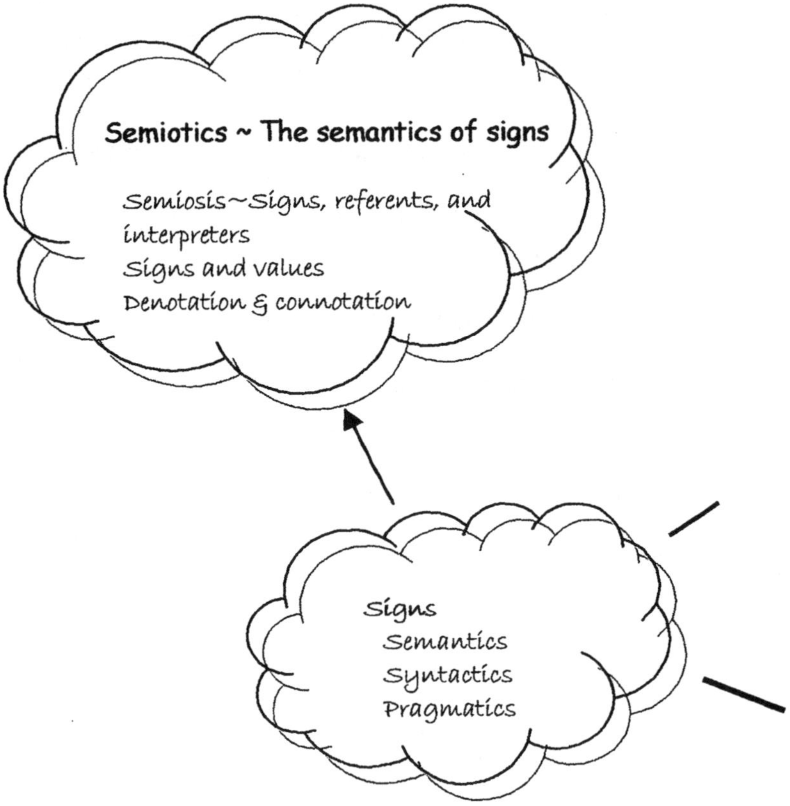

Chapter 4 Map
Theories of Signs and Language

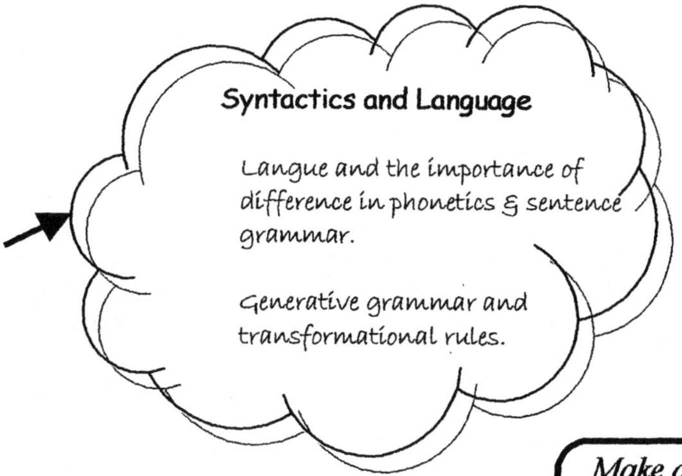

Make a Map

How would you map this chapter differently? Try it several ways and see what you learn.

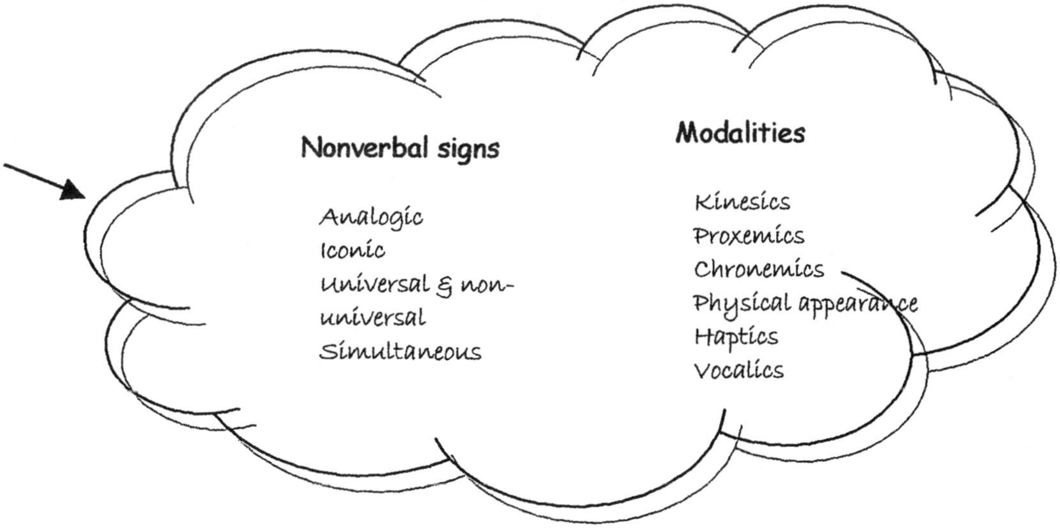

WORD PUZZLE

Below is a stair of 15 steps. Each step contains a number of spaces from 1-15. On the next page is a list of examples corresponding to each step, from top to bottom. In the chapter find an appropriate term for each step that contains exactly the same number of letters as there are spaces. In other words, the first term must have one letter; the second, two letters; the third, three; etc. You may fill in the steps in any order.

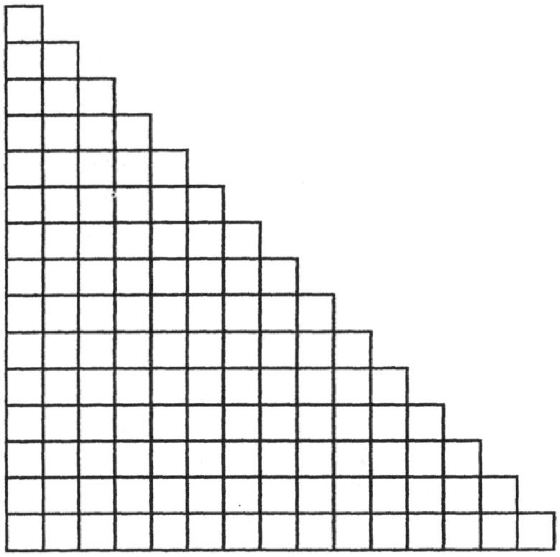

Examples

1. Any sentence.
2. John is confident and thinks nothing of his friend's insult.
3. Juanita is looking for just the right words to tell her friend that she is sorry.
4. George waves to his friend from across the park.
5. Little Lily who is just one year old loves to say, "Rrrrrrr."
6. Juanita is successful in telling her friend that she is sorry.
7. Juanita decided to tell her friend she was sorry in a letter.
8. When little Lily says, "Rrrrrrr," she points to a toy truck.
9. Being a linguist, Lily's father Pete is especially interested in this behavior of his daughter.
10. Now, whenever Lily says, "Rrrrrr," her father runs to get the truck for her.
11. Mary loves to grow roses and always has vases of roses in her house. Whenever she hears the word *rose*, she gets a good feeling and thinks of beauty.
12. Alexis gets angry when he hears a particular commercial and decides to call the station to complain.
13. When the light turns red, you had better stop.
14. In his ESL class, Vern runs through a drill: "Bob threw the ball. The ball was thrown by Bob. Did Bob throw the ball?"
15. People in every culture raise their eyebrows when they are surprised.

Answer:

S	(from Fig. 4.3)													
A	C	(from Fig. 4.2)												
U	S	E												
K	I	N	E											
P	H	O	N	E										
P	A	R	O	L	E									
M	E	S	S	A	G	E								
S	E	M	I	O	S	I	S							
S	E	M	I	O	T	I	C	S						
P	R	A	G	M	A	T	I	C	S					
C	O	N	N	O	T	A	T	I	O	N				
M	A	N	I	P	U	L	A	T	I	O	N			
S	I	G	N	I	F	I	C	A	T	I	O	N		
T	R	A	N	S	F	O	R	M	A	T	I	O	N	
S	P	E	C	I	E	S	C	O	N	S	T	A	N	T

CHALLENGES

Internet Challenges

Searching for signs: Select a site that is interesting to you. Please choose one with interesting graphics, animation, and sound.

1. As you peruse the site, look for examples of arbitrary, iconic, and intrinsic coding. Look at all aspects of the site, including language, still and animated visual images, and sounds. Notice how the signs are placed in relation to one another.
2. Notice the pragmatics of the coding. How are the signs used? What effects do you think the web designer meant to achieve?
3. How might different visitors interpret or understand these signs differently?
4. What would Suzanne Langer say about this site?

Using Your Whole Brain

Go to a place you like. This might be your room, a gym, a garden, a park, the zoo, your car, or any other place that has personal meaning to you.

Sit quietly for one hour. Do not write anything down, but just look and listen carefully. Make note of as many different signs as you can. As you look at things, notice what they stand for, what feelings they elicit in you, and how you orient to them. Notice how the various signs in the space relate to one another or how they work together to create a certain meaning for you.

How is this a semiotic space? In other words, how does this space and what is contained in it express certain meanings. What is denoted? What are your connotations? Do you view these signs with detachment, dependence, or dominance, and in what ways? In what ways do these signs designate, prescribe, or appraise?

THEORY TO ACTION

Visit a play rehearsal. Most colleges and universities have plays constantly in production, and you can get permission to sit in the audience section and watch.

Before your observation, make a checklist of nonverbal behaviors from this chapter. Watch how the director and actors make use of these behaviors in performing. Listen in as they make decisions about how to move, stand, and gesture. What effects are they trying to achieve?

CASES

My Case: The Names Project*

In November of 1985 Cleve Jones, a San Francisco activist, observed the federal building in that city covered with pieces of cardboard bearing the names of people who had died of AIDS. He realized that the world needed an AIDS memorial, and a year later under his leadership the AIDS quilt was born. By the middle of the year, forty panels had been completed. Now over 44,000 panels have been submitted to the Names Project, each devoted to a person or persons who have died of AIDS. The entire quilt has been shown several times in Washington, D. C. and elsewhere, and portions of it travel from town to town around the country. The quilt has now outgrown the entire ellipse adjacent to the White House, over fifteen acres.

Each panel, three feet by six feet, has been lovingly sewn by the friends and family of those being honored. Some individuals with AIDS have even contributed to their own quilt square. Each piece contains symbols of the person's life, and the entire quilt is a mélange of perhaps millions of symbols representing a universe of experiences. Most, though not all, squares bear the name of the individual, many have pictures, some have poetry and other writings, and sometimes certain personal objects such as a jacket have been sewn into the piece. There are squares for famous people such as Rock Hudson and Liberace and unknown people as well. Squares have been created by children for their parents, by parents for their children, by spouses, lovers, and friends.

One of the most touching squares is solid red with small images of shells, a ribbon, dogs, and cats attached. In the middle is scripted in large letters "Love you Dad." One of the simplest and most beautiful is a row of twelve red candles, three lit and nine out. In his attached statement, the creator wrote: "To the twelve men I expected to grow old with, nine who have passed on and three who will join them soon." Another square is made of baby's blankets, a pillow, and several stuffed animals. At the top, it reads simply, "Baby Jessica."

The showing of the quilt is a major event that can attracts thousands of people. It is a special event for those who knew individuals memorialized, but is an emotional and memorable event for any viewer. Usually, during a showing, the names of those represented in the quilt are read over a microphone by friends, partners, and family members.

This case is described in Cindy Ruskin, *The Quilt. Stories From the Names Project* (New York: Pocket Books, 1988).

My Analysis: The AIDS quilt is a magnificent semiotic artifact. It consists of millions of symbols representing an amazingly broad spectrum of objects, events, personalities, qualities, memories, and experiences. From a semantic perspective, the quilt squares represent many life experiences. Each square, like the entire quilt, is a composite of several signs operating together syntactically, and from a pragmatic perspective, the quilt touches people's lives in many important ways.

Because the words and objects used in the quilt are carefully considered by those who created each square and because the images in the quilt linger on in the minds of those who saw it, each square is a symbol of the lives it represents. Each is an abstraction from the life of the memorialized victim. Some of the squares include discursive symbols, but most are primarily presentational. Because of every viewer's common recognition of what the various quilt symbols represent, each square has some denotative value, but their connotations are far more significant. Indeed, the private feelings that may be aroused by images in the quilt can be extremely personal and hard to share with others in any kind of denotative way.

The quilt consists of innumerable codes because of the sign relations present for its creators and viewers. As such, the quilt is highly diachronic. Because the meanings of the various signs in the quilt are so personal and individual, one certainly could not claim that it makes use of a synchronic code system of any kind, although the quilt managers probably have a rather well developed and highly denotative code system they use among themselves to transport, assemble, and display the quilt for the public.

Virtually all of the types of signs discussed in this chapter are present in the quilt. Many of the images use ostension because they include actual objects from the person's life. When objects from a life are assembled and sewn into the quilt, the square forms a "replica" of that person's life. Almost all of the squares involve the inventive use of signs because each includes a new code created by those who made the squares.

As nonverbal communication, the quilt is an especially good illustration of proxemics, or the use of space. The quilt itself is semifixed-feature space and consists almost entirely of artifacts. To use Ekmian and Friesen's labels, we would say that the quilt is almost entirely cultural in origin; iconic and intrinsic in coding; and is communicative, interactive, and informative in usage.

Your Case and Analysis: Burger King

Visit your closest Burger King (or another fast food restaurant of your choice). Analyze the use of coding and language, including the building, its layout, the uniforms, the menu, all of the artifacts in and around the place, and any signs or other linguistic codes in use.

CRITICAL INCIDENT

The Campaign

You are a "human behavior specialist" in a large, Manhattan-based advertising firm. The agency recently landed a huge contract with Students Against Drunk Driving (SADD) to fight alcohol abuse among university students. You have been assigned to work with the team on this campaign. The campaign will make use of paid advertisements in campus publications of ail sorts.

The team decides that the initial phase of the campaign should take place over a full academic year with evaluation and redesign at the end of this period. The campaign will make use of repeated exposures of various images, and your team begins by exploring possible thematic images to employ.

Using semiotics as a base, what will you recommend and why?

Communication Theory and Scholarship

Theory in the Proce

System Theory

Theories of Signs a

Theories of Discou

Theories of Messag

Theories of Messag

Theories of Symbo

Theories of Social a

Theories of Experie

Critical Theories

Communication in Relationships

Communication in Group Decision Making

Communication in Organizational Networks

Communication and Media

Chapter 5

Theories of Discourse

- What is discourse?
- How do people use discourse to do things?
- How is discourse organized?
- How does discourse become meaningful?
- How do people have conversations?

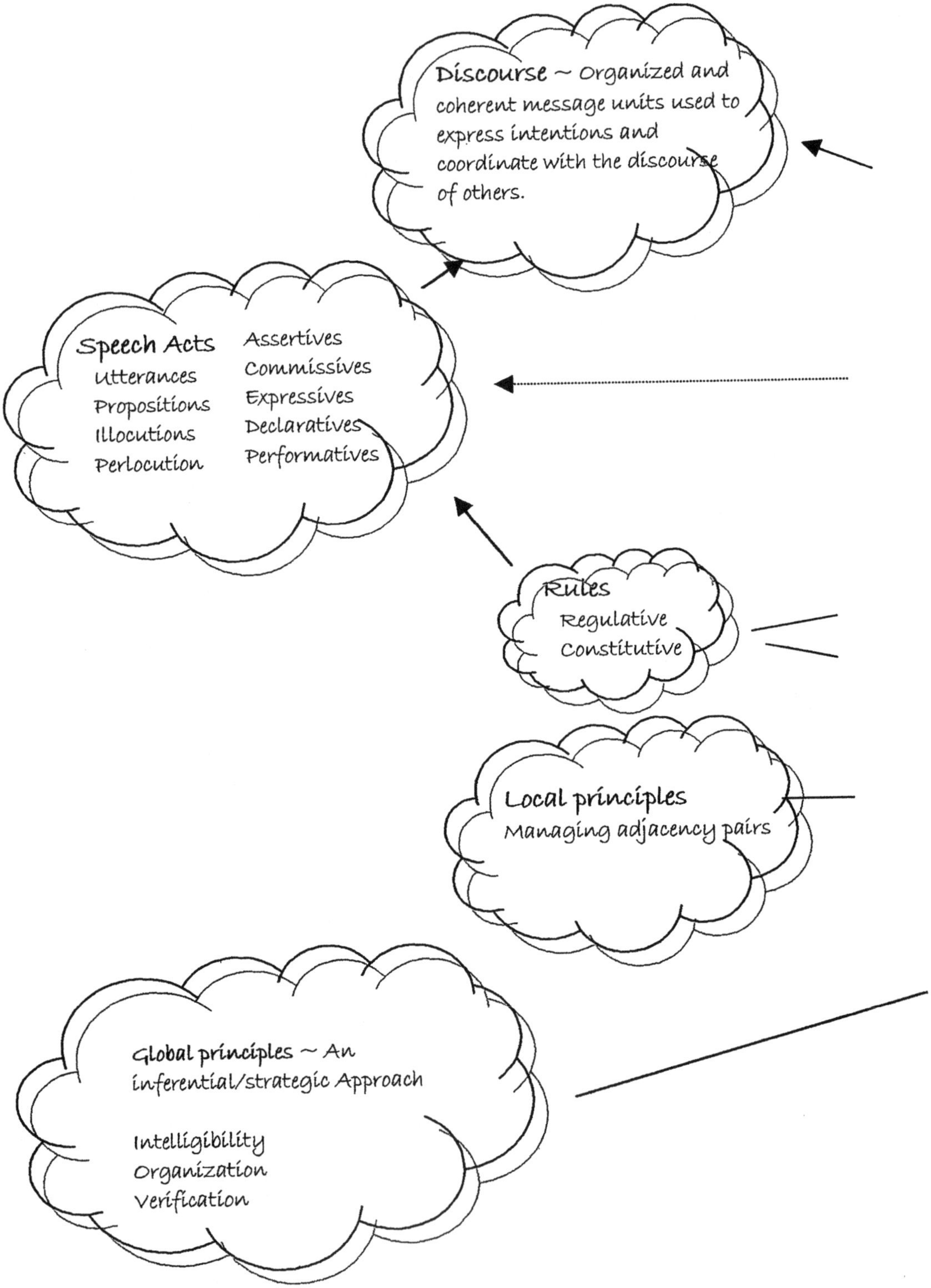
Discourse ~ Organized and coherent message units used to express intentions and coordinate with the discourse of others.
Speech Acts
Utterances
Propositions
Illocutions
Perlocution
Assertives
Commissives
Expressives
Declaratives
Performatives
Rules
Regulative
Constitutive
Local principles
Managing adjacency pairs
Global principles ~ An inferential/strategic Approach
Intelligibility
Organization
Verification

Make a Map

How would you map this chapter differently? Try it several ways and see what you learn.

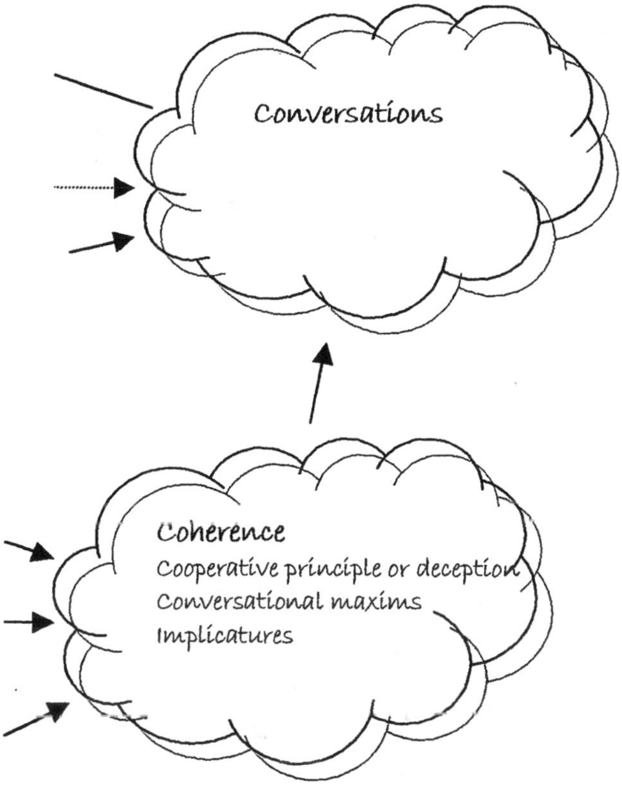

Chapter 5 Map

Theories of Discourse

WORD PUZZLE

Embedded in each statement below are the letters in order of a term from the chapter that relates to the statement itself. The object is to find the hidden word in each statement. Write the word in the space under the statement as shown in the following example:

Example

Sometimes called ***R****egulative, these guides are* ***U****sed in* ***L****anguage and oth****E****r* ***S****emiotic forms.*

Answer: R U L E S

1. Although it is not always calm, everyone assigns this in all global and local situations.

Answer:____

2. A language metaphor.

Answer:____

3. Done in order to require someone to commit to doing something you've been wanting them to do.

Answer:____

4. Maxim: One must never be deliberately unclear.

Answer:____

5. General meaning, not local, but applying to the whole conversation.

Answer:____

6. In conversational coherence, communicators put a pair between the parts of another one.

Answer:____

NOTES

Answers:

1. meaning
2. game
3. directive
4. manner
5. global
6. insertion

CHALLENGES

Internet Challenges

Imagine that you were hired by a group of discourse researchers to prepare a high-quality website on theories of discourse.

1. Do a bit of web research to see what else of this nature might have been created.

2. Create a site map. What would you put on the site and how would you link various pages?

3. Now create an actual site using your favorite web software. (Presumably, you will not actually upload the document to a host, though you might turn it in to your professor as an assignment.)

Using Your Whole Brain

With permission, audio tape several conversations. Muffle your ears and play back these conversations so that you can hear the intonation and rhythm, but not the actual words. Listen carefully to the melody and harmony of the conversations. What can you tell by listening to tone and not language? What can you learn about turn taking, speech acts, emotional content, etc.? Draw on your experience to "get the feel" of the conversation.

Now un-muffle your ears and listen again both to the language and paralanguage. Match the words with the rhythm and tone. What can you learn about conversational management by doing this?

THEORY TO ACTION

Some people are more skilled in conversational discourse than others. Skilled conversationalists have a good sense of the rules of conversation, how to take turns, how to interrupt, how to tell a story, how to flow and organize a piece of talk. People like to talk with these individuals because it is relatively easy.

As you talk with others over a period of time, evaluate how effective you and your partners seem to be. Notice awkward spots, misunderstood speech acts, miscues, and other violations.

Listen especially for the skill with which different people handle Grice's four maxims and how effectively they manage implicature.

How well do you yourself manage conversations? How can you improve your conversational skills? Frame this self-critique in terms of the theories from this chapter.

CASES

My Case: "Get Out of Bed"

Sheila: Get out of bed!

Bob: What time is it?

Sheila: Get out of bed!

Bob: [silence]

Sheila: Time to go to school.

Bob: [silence]

Sheila: It's 7:30, time to go to school.

Bob: I'm hungry.

Sheila: Milk and toast in the kitchen.

Bob: Thanks.

Sheila: Your books are by the stairs.

Bob: Okay.

Sheila: I'm off to work.

Bob: Okay, see you tonight.

Sheila: Bye.

Bob. Bye.

My Analysis: This is a simple conversation that illustrates many of the features of discourse. At base, the episode is a language game played according to rules by this mother and son. They probably both know the rules very well, and their speech acts are probably quite predictable. Because of the pattern of behavior in this episode, any member of the family could tell you that the mother is getting her son out of bed and ready for school. A set of constitutive rules makes this episode readily identifiable, and the mother and son know how to respond to one another by virtue of their regulative rules. So, for example, when Bob says he's hungry, Sheila knows that she is supposed to tell him what's for breakfast.

In telling her son to get out of bed, Sheila is using a set of perlocutionary acts, designed to affect his behavior. Sheila uses some propositions, such as, "It is 7:30, time to go to school," but these are illocutionary acts because she wants Bob to know her intention of informing him of the time and getting him ready for school. Saying that it is time to go to school is an assertive act, and telling him to get up is a directive.

This is not a very coherent conversation by local principles. If you take each turn literally, the adjacency pairs do not seem to make much sense. For example, when Sheila says, "Get out of bed," Bob says, "What time is it?" Some of Sheila's statements are even met by silence. By global standards, however, the conversation is perfectly coherent. Both parties know exactly where they are going with this conversation, the interaction is logical, and no confusion results. The quantity maxim may be violated when Bob fails to respond to his mother's initial statements, but the rules of the sequence allow silence as a way of saying, "I'm waking up and will be up in a minute." Although Sheila violates the manner maxim by using an indirect request ("It's 7:30, time to go to school."), Bob knows by implicature what is intended.

Your Case: The Tryout

Melody: Are you going to try out for the senior play this afternoon?
Jody: I dunno. I've been thinking about it.
Melody: Why not?
Jody: I might.
Melody: I am.
Jody: Well, maybe I won't,
Melody: Oh, come on.
Jody: I'm awfully busy right now.
Melody: So am I.

Jody: You were in the play last semester.
Melody: So?
Jody: I've never been in one.
Melody: So?
Jody: Well, I'll think about it.
Melody: Gotta run. See you at the tryout.

Your Analysis: Analyze this conversation using the principles discussed in this chapter. How would you explain this passage with a rule-following approach? How does your explanation change if you employ a rule-using approach? What speech acts are included in this dialogue and what are their illocutionary and perlocutionary intents? What types of speech acts are included? Is this a coherent conversation? Why? Explain coherence using both local and global principles.

CRITICAL INCIDENT

Playwriting

You are a professor of Theatre Arts at a small university. In your playwriting class, you require each student to write a one-act play as a term project. The subject and approach are left wide open, and you typically get a variety of plays to read at the end of the semester. You grade these in terms of the effectiveness of playwriting technique and creativity. You want plays that are conceptually original, but you also want to know that students understand how to use the conventions of playwriting. This is typically viewed by students as a difficult assignment.

After using this assignment for several semesters, you anticipate the kinds of problems you will see in student plays. There are several, but one of the most common difficulties is lack of coherence and realistic flow in dialogue. Often students write dialogue that is forced and unnatural, not in an artistic but in a naive way. This problem is so common that you decide to deal with it directly by providing instruction early in the course in dialogue writing.

Using principles of discourse analysis, design an instructional unit for your playwriting class that will help students write natural, coherent dialogue. Explain your material in terms of theories in Chapter 5.

Chapter 6

Theories of Message Production

- How do traits, situations, and cognition affect the ways in which we produce messages?
- How do people adjust to one another in interaction?
- What is the outcome of cognition in communication?
- To what extent and in what ways do we select or design messages?

Chapter 6 Map
Theories of Message Production

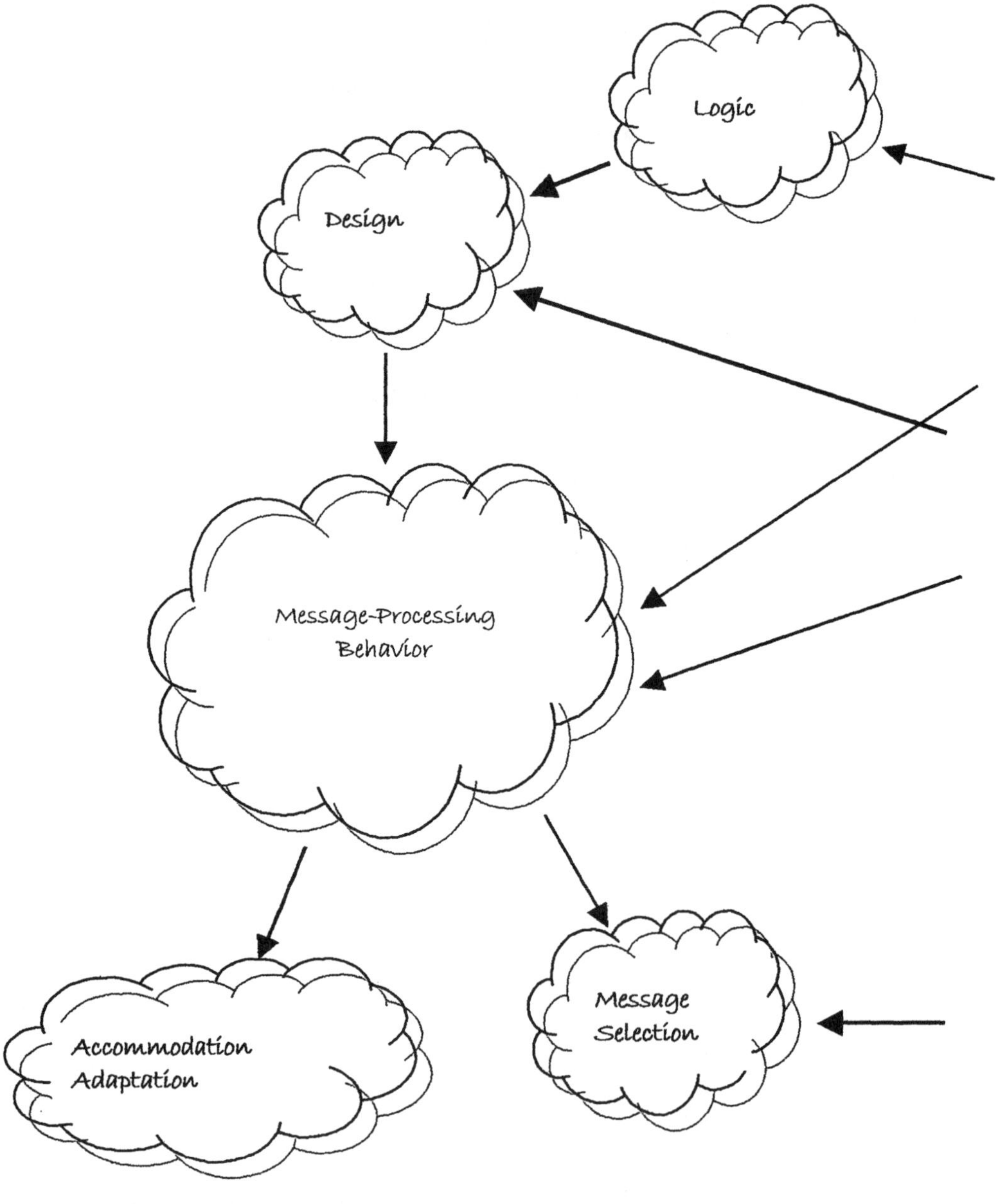

Communication Theory and Scholarship

Theory in the Proce

System Theory

Theories of Signs a

Theories of Discou

Theories of Messag

Theories of Messag

Theories of Symbol

Theories of Social a

Theories of Experie

Critical Theories

Communication in Relationships

Communication in Group Decision Making

Communication in Organizational Networks

Communication and Media

Chapter 6

Theories of Message Production

- How do traits, situations, and cognition affect the ways in which we produce messages?
- How do people adjust to one another in interaction?
- What is the outcome of cognition in communication?
- To what extent and in what ways do we select or design messages?

Chapter 6 Map
Theories of Message Production

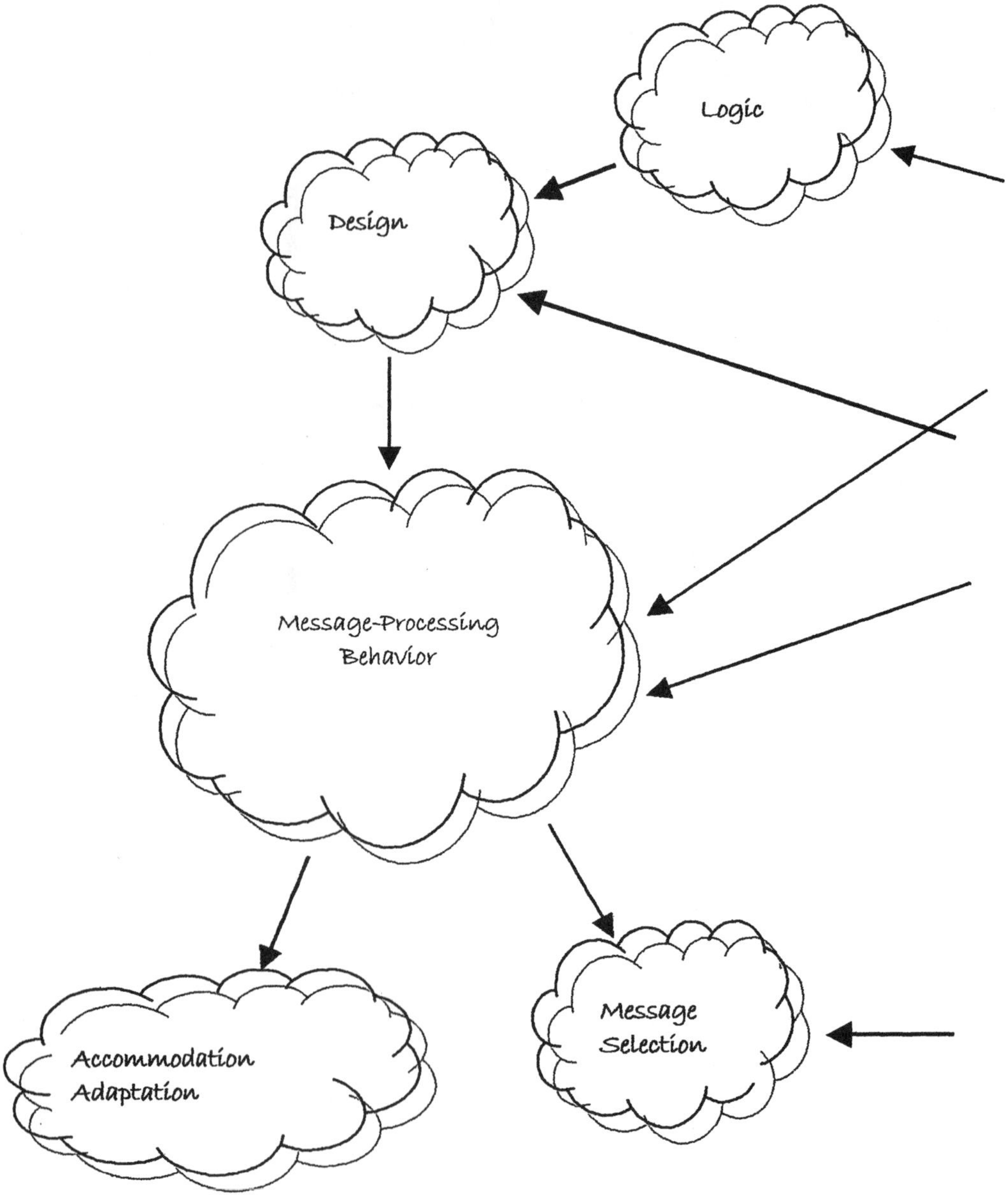

Make a Map
How would you map this chapter differently? Try it several ways and see what you learn.

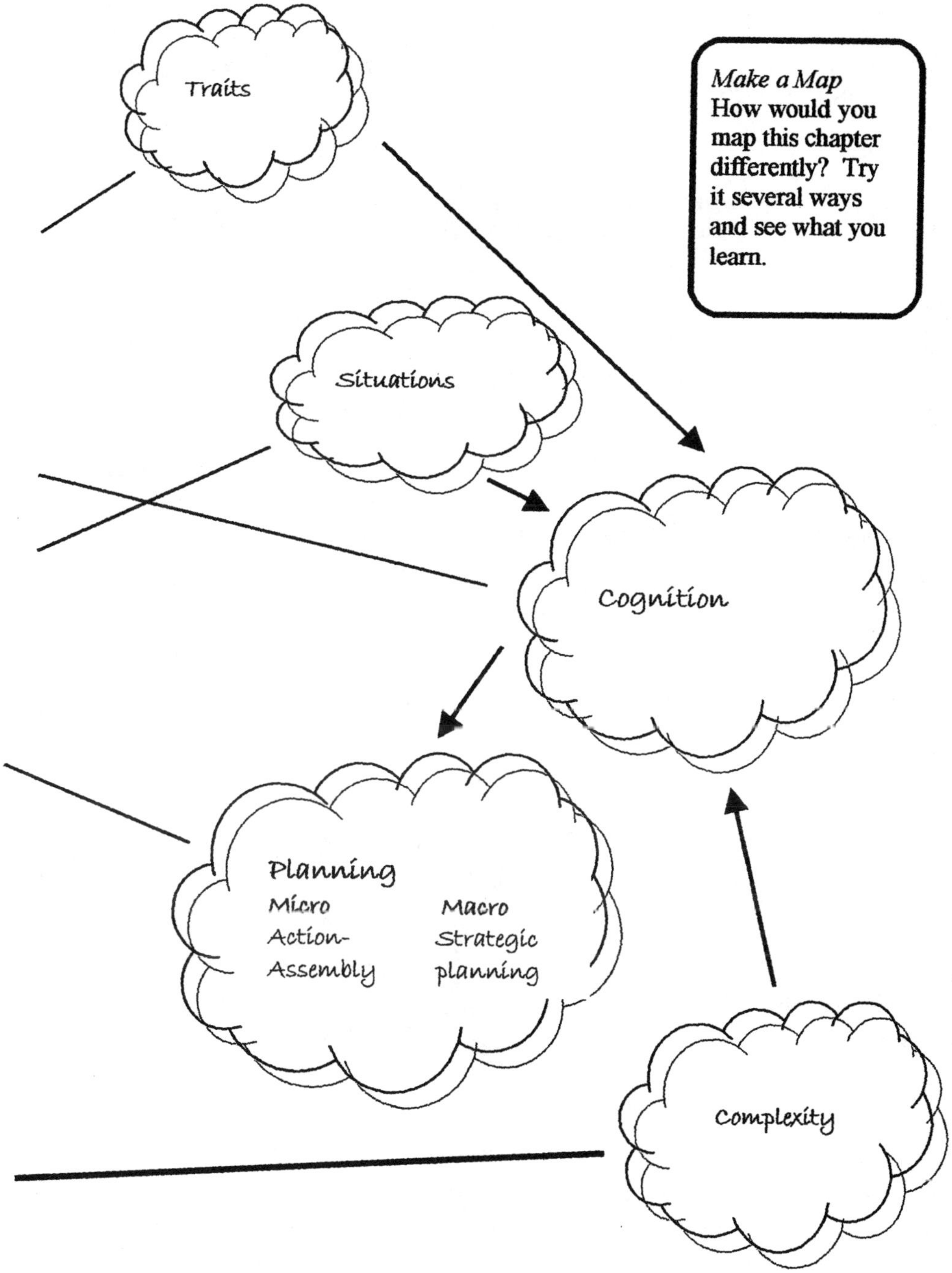

WORD PUZZLE

Below is a list of mixed-up terms from the chapter along with hints. Write the correct term in the space provided using all of the letters.

1. The ease with which one follows a plan

C A T   I N   O L D   I F U I T Y

2. Trying to get other people to do what you want them to do.

M A N   I N   P L A I N   G I C O G E C

3. Tendency to be self-absorbed in conversation.

S E N S A T I O N A L   N O R C   S A C R I V I S M

4. Pertaining to mental process.

N O   G E C I T I V

5. Theory developed by Jesse Delia and his colleagues.

M U S T   C O S T   C I V I R N

6. A basic need of all people.

C A F E

7. Thought processes behind a message.

G L O S S E N E D   M E S A   G I G I C

NOTES

Answers:

1. The ease with which one follows a plan
ACTION FLUIDITY

2. Trying to get other people to do what you want them to do.
COMPLIANCE GAINING

3. Tendency to be self-absorbed in conversation.
CONVERSATIONAL NARCISSISM

4. Pertaining to mental process.
COGNITIVE

5. Theory developed by Jesse Delia and his colleagues.
CONSTRUCTIVISM

6. A basic need of all people.
FACE

7. Thought processes behind a message.
MESSAGE DESIGN LOGIC

CHALLENGES

Internet Challenges

Visit two or three of your favorite websites. Surf through these sites carefully looking at a variety of message-design elements, including photography, sound, graphics, and language. Look also at the site architecture.

1. Quickly review action-assembly theory. Make a list of the content knowledge and procedural knowledge the designer must have had to create this site. How might these cluster together into procedural records and unitized assemblies? Correlate these to the designer's output representation.

2. Now look again at planning theory. If you were to create a website (perhaps you already have), what would be your metagoals and canned plans? What would you need to assemble into your working memory? What specific domain knowledge and general domain knowledge would you rely on?

3. Which theory works best in describing what a web designer does—a theory of message selection or a theory of message design? Why?

4. Apply constructivism to the work of a web designer.

5. Which message design logic works best for web designers?

Using Your Whole Brain

Draw visual metaphors for three theories in this chapter. You can make your drawings as elaborate or simple as you wish. If you want to use color or texture, please feel free to do so. Remember that your drawings should be metaphorical, not literal.

THEORY TO ACTION

1. Get permission to sit in on a public speaking class when students are giving persuasive speeches. (You can use your own class if you are currently enrolled in public speaking.) For each speaker, determine whether a strategy-choice or message-design model is being used. Why do you think so? What message strategies (whether selected or designed) does each speaker use?

2. Create a training session on Effective Interpersonal Communication in the Workplace. In your training, integrate concepts and practices from Accommodation Theory, Interaction Adaptation Theory, and Politeness Theory. Although you may want to explain some of these theoretical concepts, please concentrate more on the *how* implicit in these theories. Be sure to include some exercises. You may want to practice actually doing the training with a group of friends or associates.

3. An assumption of cognitive theory is that when you have to work hard mentally, you will take more time to get a job done. In other words, cognitively simple tasks are done quickly, while more complex ones take longer. Sometimes the difference is only in seconds. Over the course of one day, notice times when you get stuck in your thinking, pause to reflect, or have trouble assembling thoughts and actions. Contrast these with moments in which your responses are quick and automatic. Think about the difference in mental demands being made in these two types of situations. What types of tasks and situations are easier or more difficult for you? Why do you think this is so?

CASES

My Case: The Interview

Ms. Rogers: Let's get started right off by having you tell me what you think you can contribute to Duffey Diaper Company.

Joe: Well, first, I carefully researched the baby-products industry to find just the right company for me. And Duffey's is the best all around. I really want to work for you, Ms. Rogers.

Rogers: What do you think you can contribute?

Joe: Whatever you want from me, I can supply. I just want to do my very best.

Rogers: Okay, what skills do you bring to the job?

Joe: First, I love babies, and I really want to work in the baby industry. I'll do my very best.

Rogers: And what else?

Joe: Well, what do you think are your most important needs?

Rogers: We want a good product developer with R & D skills.

Joe: That's me. Yup. I can meet the bill.

Rogers: What kind of experience do you have?

Joe: I majored in textiles and paper engineering, and I got a minor in child development. I also worked in the child care co-op, and I got to see a lot of diapers, yes I did.

Rogers: What opinions did you form about diapers?

Joe: Duffey's is the best. All the other brands fall apart, and they don't stick very well.

Rogers: What did you think was the biggest drawback of Duffey's diapers?

Joe: No problem at all. No, they're just about perfect.

Rogers: Okay, Joe. I think that'll be enough for now. We'll be in touch.

My Analysis: In this amusing interview, Joe is trying to get a job at Duffey Diaper Company. His approach is simple: Tell them you can do the job and want to work there. The compliance-gaining strategy here seems to be positive esteem and reinforcement.

The problem is that Joe does not seem to be very person-centered in his communication and does not adapt his message very well to what Ms. Rogers might expect in an interview. He does not seem to do a very good job of perspective taking, possibly because he does not possess very high cognitive complexity. The fact that he is so vague in his black-white evaluation of diapers is further evidence for this possibility. Joe's message design logic seems to be some combination of expressive and rhetorical.

Joe does not seem particularly high in communication apprehension, and he assimilates as he gets to know Ms. Rogers's expectations. Joe also seems to be low in all aggression traits. He might be somewhat assertive, but he is certainly not argumentative in any way. When Ms. Rogers asks him how to improve Duffey's diapers, he demures.

All in all, Joe might have something to learn from this chapter.

Your Case: The Police Report

September 14, 1991

At 9:32 P.M. Officer Milford and I got a call about shouting and fighting occurring at 123 First Avenue. We arrived at the scene at 9:46. We heard no sounds coming from the house. We knocked on the door and were admitted by a woman. A man was also on the premises.
The woman identified herself as Maggie Potter, age 32. She has black hair and is medium in height. The man identified himself as George Potter, age 36, medium height, black hair. The woman was bruised around the eyes and face. The man was disheveled and sweating. The

living room was messy with tables and chairs tipped over and objects strewn about. There were several gashes and dents in the wall.

Ms. Potter sat quietly while we were there and refused to answer questions. Mr. Potter was hostile and verbally abusive to us. We took Mr. and Ms. Potter to the station for questioning. After arriving there, they calmed down and answered questions politely.

Ms. Potter said that her husband was angry because the house was messy and they were out of beer. By her account, he had told her that it was her job to take care of him and the house, and he would teach her a lesson, whereupon he slapped her and knocked her down. She said they got into a "cat and dog" fight.

Mr. Potter confirmed that he hit Ms. Potter. He showed no remorse. He said that men have the right and duty to '"take care of their wives, if you know what I mean." He said that she has gotten lazy and never keeps herself up anymore. He said that the refrigerator has been out of beer three times this week. He also said that the law has no business butting into their lives.

Mr. Potter was booked for assault at 10:56 and admitted to the jail. Ms. Potter was released to go to the hospital with her sister.

Signed,
Officer James Foster

Your Analysis: Use concepts from this chapter to discuss and explain Mr. Potter's behavior. Consider applying some of the communication traits discussed in this chapter. For example, what traits did he display? How would you characterize his accommodation behavior? What form does his interaction adaptation take? What can you say about the individual's respective action-assembly process? Does planning theory provide any insights? What message design logics are used by Mr. Potter? What does he need to learn about compliance gaining strategies? How would you characterize his cognitive differentiation, complexity, and person-centered communication? Which theories do you find most useful in your analysis?

CRITICAL INCIDENT

The Selection

Your group is the selection committee for the Aldren Fellows Program, which provides intensive training and experience for young public policy professionals. The program is designed to promote leadership and nurture talented individuals in public policy fields. The fellowship comes with a handsome stipend and living expenses for one year.

Each fellow is assigned to work as an intern with a public policy agency somewhere in the country. You try to place interns in a wide variety of agencies in every part of the country. Agencies include municipal governments, the federal government, private foundations, lobbying groups, and non-profit agencies of all types. Twice a month throughout the fellowship year, the recipients are flown to a central location to participate together in a two-day intensive training. These trainings are held in major cities around the country.

Each year you select twelve recipients. The Aldren Fellowship is a highly prestigious award, and your committee receives about ten times as many applications as positions available. You select fellows on the basis of potential for leadership in the public policy field.

Your work for this year is just about finished. You have only two more positions to fill, and you must choose from among six remaining applicants. Attempt to reach consensus on the selection of two of the following individuals. Be prepared to justify your choices on the basis of material from Chapter 6. Do not be hasty in your selection, and spend some time discussing a variety of factors from the chapter that might be useful in your selection. If you find the selection difficult, welcome to the real world!

Jeremy_Spivey--MPA 1993 (Harvard), 26 years old. Accomplishments: President of Harvard's Golden Pin Club; Captain of the Harvard Crew; Williams Scholar. Work experience: Assistant Manager of Roger's Painting Contractors; internship with Boston Metro Court mediation program. Impressions from interview: Jeremy is an affable young man. He answered all of your questions clearly but without elaboration. He seems unpretentious and intelligent, if a bit shy. The interview was fine, but a little shorter than the others. You would characterize Jeremy as reserved. He is obviously proud of his Harvard education and mentioned it several times. He asked no questions about Aldren.

Michael Armijo--Ph.D. in Political Science, 1993, University of Nebraska, age 26. Accomplishments--Published dissertation on the animal rights lobby in Washington; community recognition award from City of Lincoln for outstanding work with Habitat for Humanity; champion debater in college. Work experience: Currently Assistant Professor of Political Science at Mankato State University; long list of summer jobs and internships in college; teaching assistant in graduate school. Impressions from interview: Michael is very lively and talkative. He answered every question thoroughly and at length. Very expressive and dramatic. Asked no questions about Aldren. Didn't seem to want to leave. Spent considerable time outlining his approach to organizing.

Bette Jeffers--M.S. in Political Science, 1994, University of Texas at El Paso, age 30. Accomplishments--Voted most likely to succeed by high school class; received outstanding student leadership award in senior year at Abilene Christian College; student actor in several plays. Work experience: Worked five years as Executive Director of an adoption agency in Houston specializing in placing African American children. Impressions from interview: Friendly and relaxed. Responsive to questions. Mature and confident. A bit parochial in orientation. Asked several excellent questions about Aldren placements. Prefers a placement in southeast. Loves children.

Deborah Child--J.D., George Washington University, 1992, age 29. Accomplishments--Editor of law school journal; voted most eloquent speaker in Moot Court, 1991; recipient of Navajo Youth Encouragement Scholarship in college. Work experience: Clerk for Justice Bryan, Fifth Circuit Federal Court; Associate in Clark, Brennan, Warren, and O'Connor (2 years). Impressions from interview: Extremely articulate and confident in presentation. Somewhat equivocal. Displayed much prior knowledge of the Aldren program. Committed to the advancement of Navajo people. Cosmopolitan tone. Flexible. Seemed to establish immediate rapport with committee members.

Anthony Bessey--Ph.D. in public administration, University of Colorado, 1994, age 31. Accomplishments--winner student essay contest, junior year of college; raised $50,000 for Denver Summer Arts Festival. Work experience: Director of small art center in Ft. Collins (3 years); student curator of university museum and gallery (4 years in college); volunteer coordinator of Denver Summer Arts Festival (2 years). Impressions from interview: Clear, but curt. Very intelligent. Open to any aspect of public administration, but most interested in the arts. Went through a long list of well outlined questions about the program. A networker. Persuasive.

Hazel Fortus--M.A. in communication, University of Arkansas, 1994, age 25. Accomplishments--participated in seven National Issues Forums throughout Arkansas; attended NIF institute in Chicago; participated in the Listening Project to mobilize residents of inner city Memphis to improve the condition of their neighborhood; participated in Detroit Summer, a college-student work project to fix and remodel dilapidated houses in downtown Detroit. Work experience: work study. Impressions from interview: Quiet and reserved, but responsive. Answers clear, but not elaborated. Committed to helping the urban poor. Hard worker. No questions. Short interview. Unable to get a clear impression of her personality.

Communication Theory and Scholarship

Theory in the Proce

System Theory

Theories of Signs a

Theories of Discou

Theories of Messag

Theories of Messag

Theories of Symbo

Theories of Social a

Theories of Experie

Critical Theories

Communication in Relationships

Communication in Group Decision Making

Communication in Organizational Networks

Communication and Media

Chapter 7

Theories of Message Reception & Processing

- How does the mind work in assigning meaning to messages?
- How is information organized cognitively, and how does that organization affect attitudes, beliefs, values, and behaviors?
- What judgment processes affect our processing of information and messages?

Make a Map
How would you map this chapter differently? Try it several ways and see what you learn.

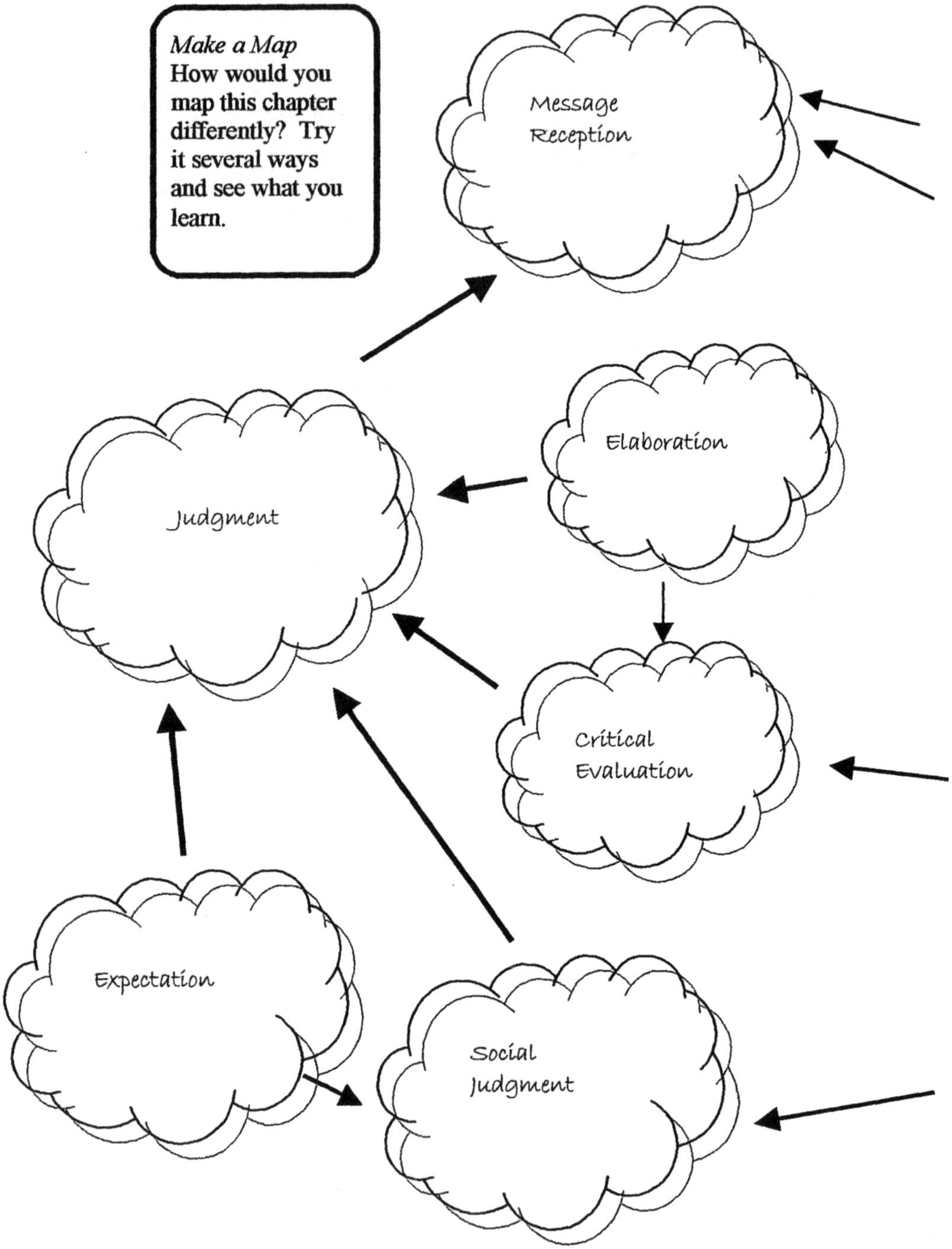

WORD PUZZLE

Below is a list of terms from the chapter with missing letters. Based on the hint, fill in the blanks.

1. Mental operations

C _ _ N _ _ _ _ E   _ _ E _ _ T _ O _ S

2. Place of meaning

_ _ _ A N _ _ _   S _ A _ _

3. Common mistake

F _ N _ _ _ _ N _ _ L   _ _ T _ _ B _ T I _ _   _ R R _ _

4. Determines behavior

_ _ A S _ _ E D   _ C _ I _ _

5. Most important beliefs.

C _ _ _ _ _ L

6. Judgment regions

L _ _ I _ U _ _ S

7. Wanting to believe

T R _ _ _   _ I A _

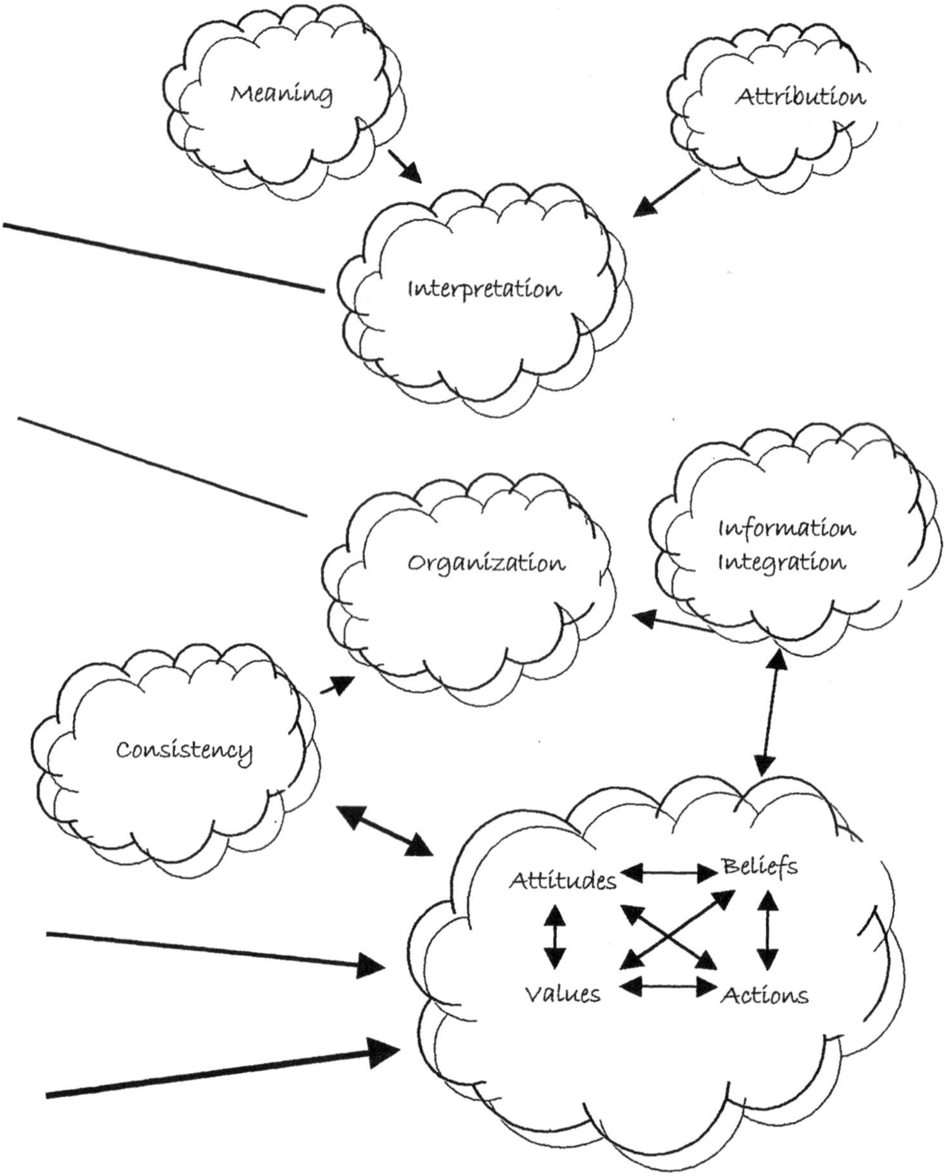

Chapter 7 Map
Theories of Message Reception and Processing

NOTES

Answers:

1. Mental operations
C O G N I T I V E   O P E R A T I O N S

2. Place of meaning
S E M A N T I C   S P A C E

3. Common mistake
F U N D A M E N T A L   A T T R I B U T I O N   E R R O R

4. Determines behavior
R E A S O N E D   A C T I O N

5. Most important beliefs.
C E N T R A L

6. Judgment regions
L A T I T U D E S

7. Wanting to believe
T R U T H   B I A S

CHALLENGES

Internet Challenges

1. Do a search for "semantic differential." How many hits did you get? Explore some of these sites and see what you learn.

2. Do a search on [+attitude +change]. How many hits did you get? Now use concepts from this chapter to narrow the search. What do you find?

3. Do a search on [+persuasion +syllabus]. You should hit on a bunch of courses on persuasion. Browse through these and see if you can tell whether or not they are using any of the theories from this chapter.

Using Your Whole Brain

Select several things that have meaning for you. These might include a song, a painting, a place, a piece of clothing, a friend or other person, a pet. How would you place your meaning for these objects within Osgood's semantic space below?

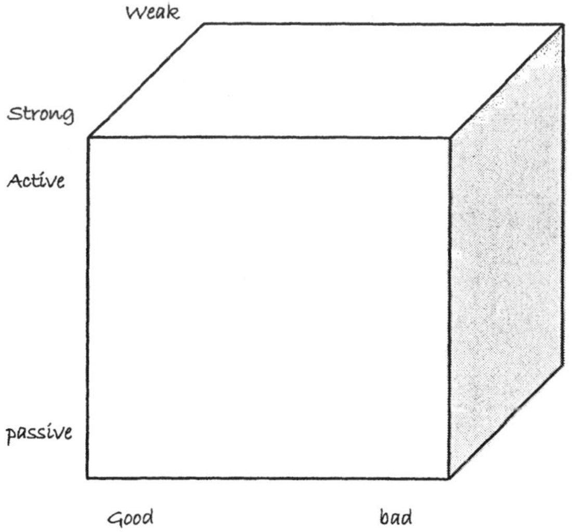

THEORY TO ACTION

If you were an attorney in a jury-selection process, how might you use each of the following processes to accept or eliminate potential jury members?

1. Attribution
2. Information integration
3. Cognitive dissonance
4. Elaboration likelihood
5. Expectancy violation
6. Interpersonal deception

CASES

My Case: When Prophecy Fails*

Sometime in the early 1950s, a small band of believers in the United States predicted that a great flood would come over the earth and completely change the face of the planet as we know it. Everybody would die except a few true believers who would be spirited off into outer space by flying saucers to be spiritually trained on a far-off planet and returned to lead the new utopian earth.

This prophecy was based on a belief system developed over a period of years primarily through the automatic writings of a psychic housewife, Mrs. Keech. Jesus Christ, who had evolved on another planet and now had the name of Sananda, periodically took control of the writer's arm and wrote messages to her. A former missionary and his wife, Dr. and Mrs. Armstrong, became aware of this event and became good friends and co-leaders in the movement, which came to be known as The Seekers. Over a period of months before the predicted demise of the earth, the group of believers grew, and in the end perhaps fifteen highly committed members had become involved.

The group believed, among other things, that beings, called the Guardians, from a planet named Clarion had visited the earth in flying saucers. Their purpose was to gather together those who were spiritually ready, alter the world, and install a new leadership. Sananda announced that the cataclysm was to occur at 5:30 A.M. on December 21. The believers prepared themselves to be transported by spacecraft either to a safe location on the earth or to another planet. They had to remove all metal from their clothes because Sananda has written that metal would cause severe burns in a flying saucer.

There were two false calls four days before the fated day. The first was a telephone call received by Mrs. Keech on December 17 from Captain Video instructing her to be ready to be picked up by a flying saucer at 4:00 that afternoon. After the saucer failed to show up, the group realized that it was just a drill. About 11:30 that evening Mrs. Keech got another message saying the spacecraft would land in her back yard that very night to pick up the chosen ones, and that everybody better be ready. The group huddled in the cold yard for several hours, but to no avail. Again, another drill. Finally, a few days later, Sananda told Mrs. Keech quite clearly that the group would be transported at 12:00 midnight on

December 21, before the flood occurred the following morning. A Guardian would knock on the door, lead the members to parked cars, and transport them to another location, where they would board spacecraft and be taken into outer space.

The group waited anxiously to the stroke of midnight for a knock at the door. The spaceman never showed up, and the group was faced with the task of justifying why the prophecy had failed. At 4:45 A.M., Keech received another message from Sananda saying that the flood had been called off because of the strength and faith of the believers. The various members of the group immediately called the press to tell them the good news and to spread the word about how their beliefs had been confirmed.

*This case is described in detail by Leon Festinger, Henry W. Riecken, and Stanley Schachter, *When Prophecy Fails* (Minneapolis: University of Minnesota Press, 1956).

My Analysis: This is an interesting case of a strongly held belief system and the actions taken by the adherents in fulfilling their beliefs. Because of their ego-involvement in the prophecy, self-beliefs were tightly connected to beliefs about the mystical, automatic writing, messages from outer space, the Guardians, and Sananda. Rokeach would agree that these were central beliefs that would be hard to change.

It is fascinating to see how information was repeatedly integrated into the belief system and how positive attitudes toward the Guardians and their prophecy developed. The believers were not afraid of the cataclysm, and indeed embraced it enthusiastically. Virtually every piece of information received by the group, including potentially disconfirming events, were incorporated into the system so as to avoid dissonance and build positive attitudes toward the predicted events.

Most of the members of the group shared a strong set of meanings. Sananda, for example, was seen as good (evaluation), very powerful (potency), and quite active (activity). Originally, Mrs. Keech was seen as good, not powerful by herself, and even somewhat passive, although later she became much more personally involved.

The case is rife with attributions. The group constantly asked why certain things happened or did not happen. They granted extreme personal causation to the Guardians, and they saw their own actions very much as situationally caused.

It is hard to tell how much cognitive processing occurred through central as opposed to peripheral routes. Although on the face it appeared that the group was not engaged in critical thinking, they often did ponder, discuss, weigh evidence, and seem to act in ways consistent with central processing. At these times they probably were processing centrally, using the belief system available to them as a framework for such processing. At other times they definitely took things at face value based on the credibility of Mrs. Keech, Dr. Amstrong, and Sananda, which is a sign of peripheral processing.

Because of their strong beliefs and high ego-involvement, the Seekers had a rather narrow latitude of acceptance and a wide latitude of rejection. Only a small number of interpretations were privileged in the thought system, and nonbelievers were dismissed out of hand as not spiritually ready. For this reason, attempts to change the group's belief system and even disconfirming happenings boomeranged to make the group's beliefs even stronger.

In sum, the case shows the power of cognition to shape reality and guide actions.

Your Case and Analysis: Self Analysis

Your case for this chapter is yourself. Choose a topic you feel strongly about and make a list of several important beliefs you have about this topic. How do these beliefs cluster into attitudes? Which of your values are relevant to this topic, and how do they affect your attitudes? Where do you get information about this topic? Think of cases in which information has bolstered your attitudes and cases in which it has shaken them. How wide or narrow are your latitudes of acceptance, noncommitment, and rejection on this topic? Do you think you distort messages and information because of these latitudes?

Make a list of several concepts (physical objects, persons, or ideas) related to this topic and discuss your meanings for them. You may want to use Osgood's semantic space as a guide. In other words, to what extent do you see these objects as good or bad, powerful or weak, active or passive?

Think about your actions in regard to the topic. What causes you to behave in these ways? What are the actions of other people and what causes these? Think of a situation involving this topic in which something happened to you and explain why you think it happened. What causal attribution processes are you using? Are you guilty of the fundamental attribution error?

Conduct a dissonance analysis of your attitudes, beliefs, values, and actions on this topic. Do you think they are consistent with one another? Do you think they are consistent with attitudes, beliefs, values, and actions on other topics? How ego-involved are you in this topic, and how closely are your beliefs tied into your self-concept? What would it take to change any of your beliefs, and what would the consequences be?

CRITICAL INCIDENT

Teenage Smoking

Smoking is spreading among adolescents. How can this trend be reversed? Use the theories from Chapter 7 to suggest ways of stopping the spread of smoking among young people.

Communication Theory and Scholarship

Theory in the Proce

System Theory

Theories of Signs a

Theories of Discou

Theories of Messag

Theories of Messag

Theories of Symbo

Theories of Social a

Theories of Experie

Critical Theories

Communication in Relationships

Communication in Group Decision Making

Communication in Organizational Networks

Communication and Media

Chapter 8

Theories of Symbolic Interaction, Structuration, and Convergence

- How is meaning made socially?
- What is the relationship of self to other?
- How does interaction lead to social structure?
- How does meaning come to be shared, and what are the consequences of shared meaning?

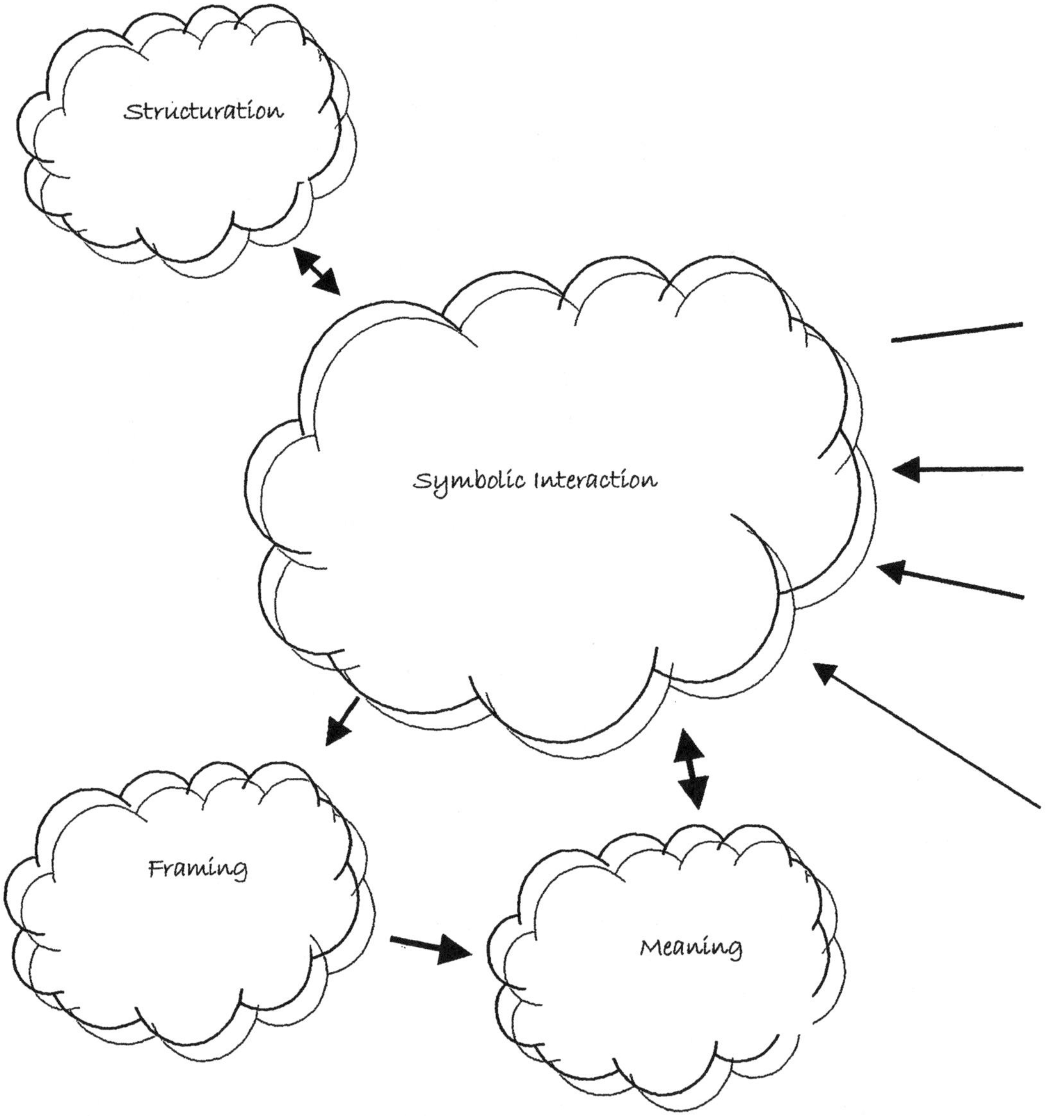

Chapter 8 Map
Theories of Symbolic Interaction, Structuration, and Convergence

Make a Map
How would you map this chapter differently? Try it several ways and see what you learn.

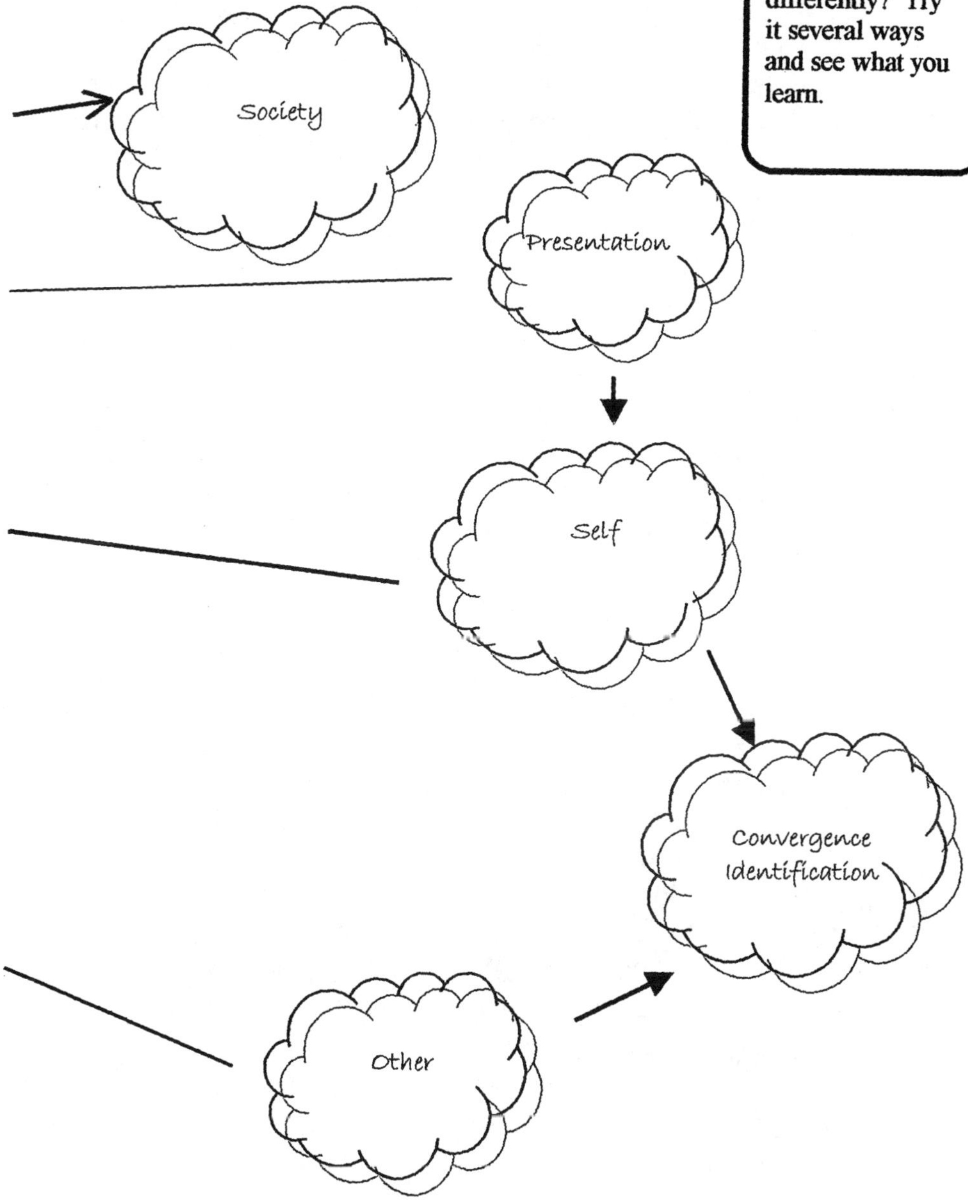

WORD PUZZLE

Below is a list of terms from the chapter. Select the correct definition in each case.

1. Chicago School
   A. A well-known school specializing in communication.
   B. One school of thought in symbolic interactionism.
   C. School of acting in which Erving Goffman gained fame.
   D. The unintended consequence of educational reform in Illinois.

2. Structuration
   A. Producing unintended consequences that shape future action.
   B. A highly stylized genre of media.
   C. Another term for symbolic interaction.
   D. Identification, or convergence.

3. Action
   A. Opposed to motion, behavior with intent and meaning.
   B. What it takes to form the self.
   C. A concept attributable primarily to Herbert Blumer.
   D. Similarity between two people.

4. Agency
   A. The result of structuration.
   B. A sense of otherness.
   C. The means, or vehicle, used to carry out an act.
   D. The presentational self.

5. Significant Other
   A. A lover, wife, husband, or fiancé.
   B. Orientational other.
   C. The person chosen to fill out a 20-statements test.
   D. Anyone with whom you experience identification.

6. Mind
   A. Opinion.
   B. Brain.
   C. Wisdom.
   D. Thinking.

NOTES

Answers:

1. B
2. A
3. A
4. C
5. B
6. D

CHALLENGES

Internet Challenges

Go back over the history of the e-mail you have exchanged with a group of colleagues, family, or friends. Check your "sent" file, "deleted file," and any other active files you maintain in your e-mail program. As you peruse this old mail, look for answers to the following questions:

1. To what extent and in what ways have these correspondents been significant others to you?
2. What joint actions did you create with these correspondents?
3. What generalized other has been formed with this group?
4. Describe your presentation of self.
5. What unintended consequences were produced?
6. What strategies of identification were used?
7. What fantasy themes were chained out?

Using Your Whole Brain

Write a rhyming poem using concepts from this chapter. The following might be a beginning:

Mead and Burke and Goffman too
Followed a path to a symbol zoo.
Self and other, back and forth
Leads to meaning, mind, and morph

THEORY TO ACTION

Take the Twenty-Statements test. Analyze it in terms of the order and locus variables. Now ask several other important orientational others to do the test for you by listing 20 items in response to the statement *You are . . .*

Compare the results of these various responses about who you are. How do these compare to the results of your own test? What aspects of a generalized other do you see in this analysis?

How do you like the results of these various versions of the test? What changes would you like to make in response to these? How would you begin to make these changes from a symbolic interactionist perspective?

CASES

My Case: The Assassination of a National Leader*

On March 16, 1978, Aldo Moro, the prime minister of Italy, was kidnapped, and his five bodyguards were killed. Fifty-five days later, Moro was murdered.

Aldo Moro was perhaps the most well-known political figure in Italy, having been prime minister five times during his lengthy career. Various interest groups, mostly in Italy, had to make sense out of his murder and in the process of doing so created a social drama. The groups included the Christian Democratic Party, the largest and most powerful party in Italy, of which Moro was president; the Italian Communist Party, the chief opposition to the Christian Democrats; the Socialist Party, a humanitarian party that was never very popular or influential; the Red Brigade, the secretive ultra-left terrorist organization responsible for the kidnapping and assassination; Moro and the Moro family; the press; and the Vatican.

Moro was kidnapped on his way to parliament where an historic vote was to take place over a coalition government. A long and heated debate was expected, but after the kidnapping the coalition government passed immediately with little debate. Even Christian Democrats who should have opposed the new government voted in favor of it because they did not want to look as if the terrorists had caused a rift in the government.

There were mass demonstrations the afternoon of the kidnapping, including a huge strike organized by the labor unions. The demonstrations were represented by the media as spontaneous and unanimous, but they really were quite well orchestrated, and many workers did not have much of a choice about participating. For the politicians, the strike was a show of unity; for the workers it was a show of sympathy for the working class body guards, who were killed in the kidnapping; for the union leaders it was good publicity.

All of the major protagonist groups took immediate positions on the issue of negotiating for Moro's return. The two leading parties, the media, and the Vatican opposed negotiating, while the Moro family, the humanitarian Socialist Party, and the Red Brigade favored it. Moro himself vigorously argued for negotiation because his life depended on it.

Of those who opposed negotiation, the Christian Democrats did not want to give official recognition to the Red Brigade, and the Communists had their own reputation to look out for and wanted to avoid the impression that they supported the terrorists in any way. For the latter group, the issue was crucial because they had just received legitimization by the newly passed coalition government. They were especially concerned about a U.S. reaction in which the terrorist Red Brigade and communists would be put together as one cause. The Socialists wanted to negotiate because of their humanitarian ideals, and the Red Brigade wanted negotiations primarily to legitimate their case.

Over the fifty-five days that Moro was in confinement, a social drama unfolded. Each group created its own way of understanding what was going on and through interaction gave structure to the events they encountered. The press told the story as various groups released statements and made demands. The mass media provided the stage for the struggle among the various interest groups, the stage on which the drama would unfold. For example, the Pope wrote a letter to the terrorists pleading for a humanitarian act of release. Moro himself wrote numerous letters urging the government to negotiate with the Red Brigade, which they steadfastly refused to do. Numerous speeches, letters, and press reports were issued during the period.

The mainstream view throughout the crisis was that to negotiate with the Red Brigade would grant this group some sort of official recognition, which would create a far more difficult and historically profound situation. In the end, Moro was made a sacrifice to the larger goal of maintaining the definition of terrorists as illegitimate and marginal.

Several key symbols and meanings functioned to define the situation in Italy during this crisis and affected the ultimate decision not to negotiate. Three of these will suffice as examples—the resistance, democracy, and the sanctity of human life.

The resistance, an anti-fascist movement during World War 11, had taken on epic symbolic value in Italy. Many believed that to negotiate with terrorists would desecrate this ideal. This overarching concept stood for everything valued in Italian government, including sacrifice, humanity, struggle, and democracy.

Another key symbol was *democracy* itself, which symbolized gradual, nonviolent change. It symbolized popular participation in government, civil liberty, and representative government. A world view marked by such ideals should have nothing to do with a band of outlaws who would capture the nation's leaders. The ideals on which the entire society is based must not be sacrificed for the life of one of the citizens of the society.

On the other side of the negotiation issue was the symbol of the sanctity of human life. In essence the life of one person symbolizes the humanity of the entire society, and the humanity of society is reflected in the lives of each citizen. This symbol was powerful for the ultra-left groups and for the Socialists, who argued in favor of negotiation.

The episode ended with Moro's death. His body was found in the trunk of a Renault on a small street in Rome. A state funeral was held in the Great Basilica of San Giovanni with Pope Paul presiding. Moro himself was an important symbol throughout the episode. Based on the ways in which he was addressed in the various communications released during this period, the Moro symbol seemed to move through four phases. Before the kidnapping, he was considered to be a secular character, a highly moral leader. Right after the kidnapping, however, he was muddled in a problematic situation for the state, losing the sense of purity in his leadership, but gaining a sacredness not before seen. In the following weeks in his letters, Moro was seen as a mortal begging for his life, unwilling to allow himself to be a sacrifice for higher ideals. Here he lost both the purity of leadership and sacredness of religious ideals. Finally, after his death Moro regained the symbol of a lost and noble leader and took on the mantle of the sacred as well.

My Analysis: This case is an excellent example of how society is itself a product of symbolic interaction. Individuals and groups, through their interlinkages, created a way of understanding and dealing with the crisis. More accurately, there were several ways of understanding and dealing with it being played out on the stage created by the press. Central to the meanings that arose during this period were significant symbols such as the resistance, democracy, the sanctity of human life, and even Moro himself.

Various rhetorical visions arose during the period, and these were influenced by fantasy themes already well chained out in Italy about the resistance movement during the war, the way in which the government operated in Italy, and other concerns. Moro had his own vision and fantasy themes which he used to try to gain coherence with the government during his captivity.

The episode itself was a series of social acts. The kidnapping, the government response, the strike, the Moro letters, the Red Brigade's demands, the Pope's communication, the assassination, and the funeral were all acts rife with symbols and attendant meanings worked out interactionally in the social drama. In Kuhn's terms, plans of action were prepared, and these were heavily influenced by people's attitudes toward social objects such as the Red Brigade, Moro, and the state.

The case is also a study of identification and the ways in which various groups attempt to achieve identification within the group and between groups. Surely Moro in his letters was struggling to develop sympathy on the part of government leaders so that they would acquiesce on the negotiating issue. The Pope's letter was an attempt to establish identification with the terrorists to persuade them to release Moro. These acts were tricky because they had also to express a certain amount of division at the same time, so that the Pope, for example, could not appear to be condoning the terrorists in his plea to them.

There was, of course, a good deal of division between protagonists during the period. Although for a moment at the funeral everyone seemed to come together, there had been a struggle to define the situation and control the way in which the government would respond. This division was not based strictly on the various positions of the groups involved in the Moro affair, but had deep roots in their political goals and situations.

Although Goffman deals primarily with individual's definitions of the situation, it is clear that groups define situations also, and the kidnapping cried out for interpretation. One of the first things the protagonist groups had to do was to define the situation. Then, they had to decide how to respond, which in large measure was a form of impression management. They hoped that by giving the impression that they would not give in that the terrorists would see the futility of their act.

*This case is elaborted in detail by Robin Erica Wagner-Pacifici, *The Moro Morality Play: Terrorism as Social Drama* (Chicago: University of Chicago Press, 1986).

Your Case: Iteso Beer Drinking*

The Iteso are a people residing near the Kenya-Uganda border near Lake Victoria in eastern Africa. Beer drinking is central to the culture and permeates almost all aspects of Iteso life. The people have their own reed straws, which they carry around from house to house in hollow poles. Not everybody drinks beer, but virtually everybody attends beer parties, which are commonly held during the harvesting season when beer is plentiful.

Although a variety of types of beer are made, the preferred is finger millet beer, which is a gruel made from flour that has been wrapped in leaves, buried for a week, and baked in a pan over a fire. It ferments for at least four days before being drunk. The Iteso customarily drink the beer from a common pot, using their own individual straws.

The Iteso have developed a vocabulary related to beer. They have words for such things as 'pouring hot water into a beer pot" and "cleaning a beer straw." Even greetings include beer references, such as: "Hello. How are you? Where is the beer?" Neighbors are defined as people with whom you share beer.

Funerals are year-long ceremonies with several stages, each symbolized by a particular type of beer preparation and drinking. These are called the "beer of the bathing," the "beer of return to work," the "beer of the hindlegs," the "beer of the forelegs," and the "beer of the funeral sacrifice."

Morals are often defined in terms of beer. For example, a good person is congenial and sociable, *epaparone,* and drinks beer with others, while bad persons are *epog,* drinking beer by themselves. This shows that sociability is an important value of the Iteso. Generosity is defined in terms of one's willingness to share beer.

The Iteso enjoy the intoxicating quality of beer, but they do not permit drunkenness, which indicates *amerit*, or loss of control, for in their environment control is very important for survival.

The following story told by an Iteso man illustrates the importance of beer in this society. The story is paraphrased as follows:

> I had a beer drinking party at my house in October for the five boys who helped me fix my house. We started drinking about 8:00 P.M., and we sat on chairs by my bed. The parents of the boys showed up and so did my parents. Some wives also came, and they sat on empty sacks on the floor.
>
> We chose Mr. Augustine to coordinate the conversation, and nobody was allowed to speak without permission from him. If anybody spoke out of turn, they had to take their straw out of the beer for a while. If anybody wanted to go out, they had to leave their straw by the pot and they could not walk between the straw and the pot; that's a rule. When a person came back in, they had to thank everybody before sitting down again. People had to ask permission before they could leave for the evening.
>
> There was music, and people were allowed to dance. My wife especially liked Mr. Otwane's dancing, so she gave him a basket full of beer flour as a reward. The drinking and dancing went on all night. When morning came, I got a chicken for the men to slaughter, and we roasted it and ate it. Later we had breakfast. They asked permission to leave, I released them, and we said goodbye.

*This case is discussed by Ivan Karp, "Beer Drinking and Social Experience in an African Society," in *Explorations in African Systems of Thought,* ed. Ivan Karp and Charles S. Bird (Washington, D. C.: Smithsonian Institution Press, 1980), pp. 83-119.

Your Analysis: As you analyze this case consider the following questions: What are the Iteso meanings for various beer-drinking rituals, and how are these meanings reinforced through interaction? How do Iteso interactions lead to the structure of Iteso society? What are some of the significant symbols associated with beer drinking? How is beer drinking involved in plans of action? How can beer drinking be understood in terms of the theory of Kenneth Burke? How can it be understood in terms of frame analysis?

CRITICAL INCIDENT

The Youth Center

You are on the Board of Directors of Youth, Inc., a non-profit organization that serves the young people of your community. Youth, Inc. operates a recreation and education center for teenagers (13-19) and targets youth at risk, especially school dropouts. Your purpose is to offer constructive experiences for adolescents, a healthy place for youth to gather, and programs to improve the lives of troubled young people.

The Board and staff realize that the chief problem of the young people you serve is self-esteem. Basically, your clients do not see themselves as successful individuals and do not imagine positive futures.

What can you do to help change this state of affairs? Use theories from this chapter to help formulate ideas.

Communication Theory and Scholarship

Theory in the Proce

System Theory

Theories of Signs a

Theories of Discou

Theories of Messag

Theories of Messag

Theories of Symbo

Theories of Social and Cultural Reality

Theories of Experience and Interpretation

Critical Theories

Communication in Relationships

Communication in Group Decision Making

Communication in Organizational Networks

Communication and Media

Chapter 9

Theories of Social and Cultural Reality

- What is real?
- How does communication work in the social construction of reality?
- How are language and culture related to one another?

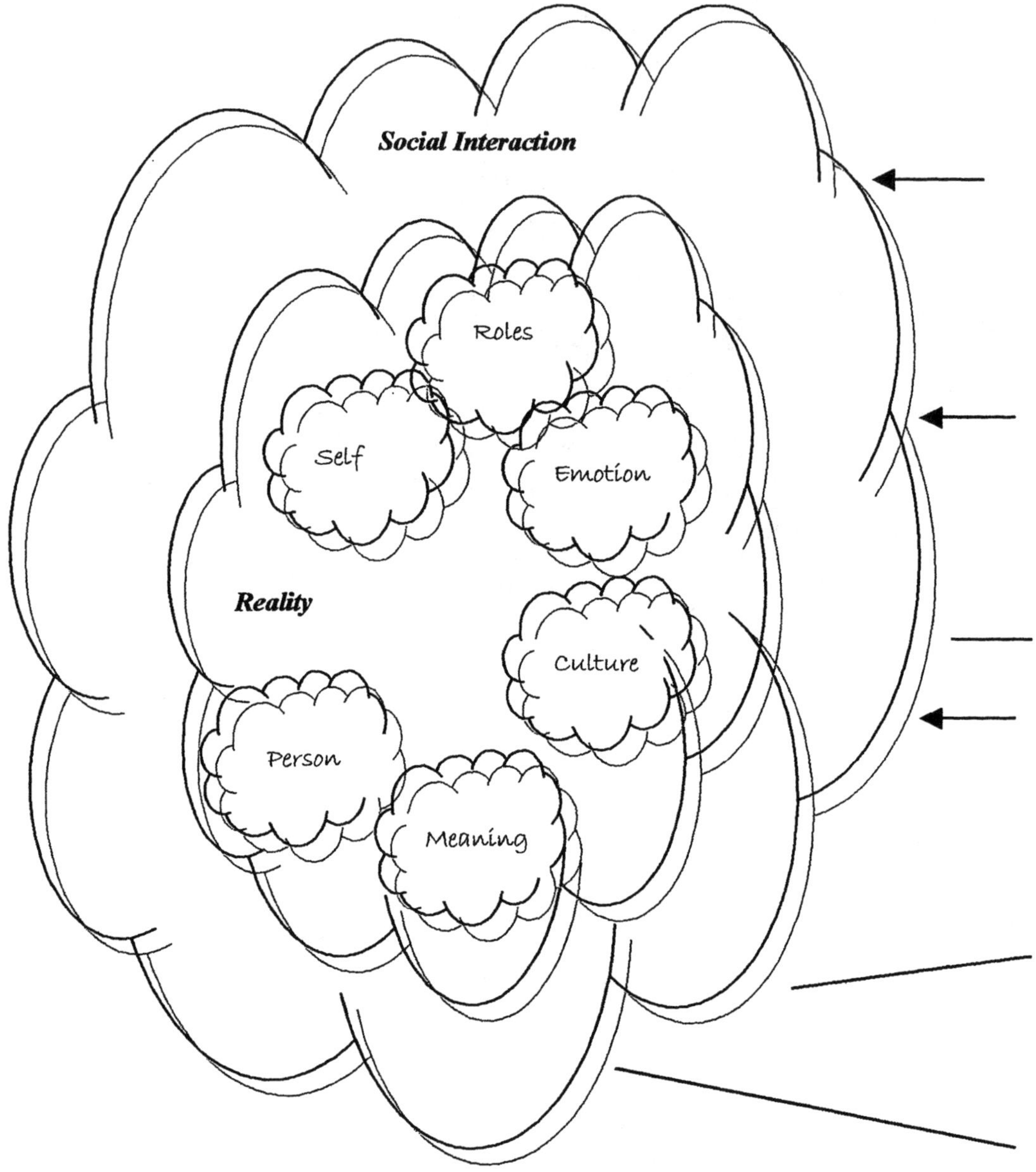

Chapter 9 Map
Theories of Social and Cultural Reality

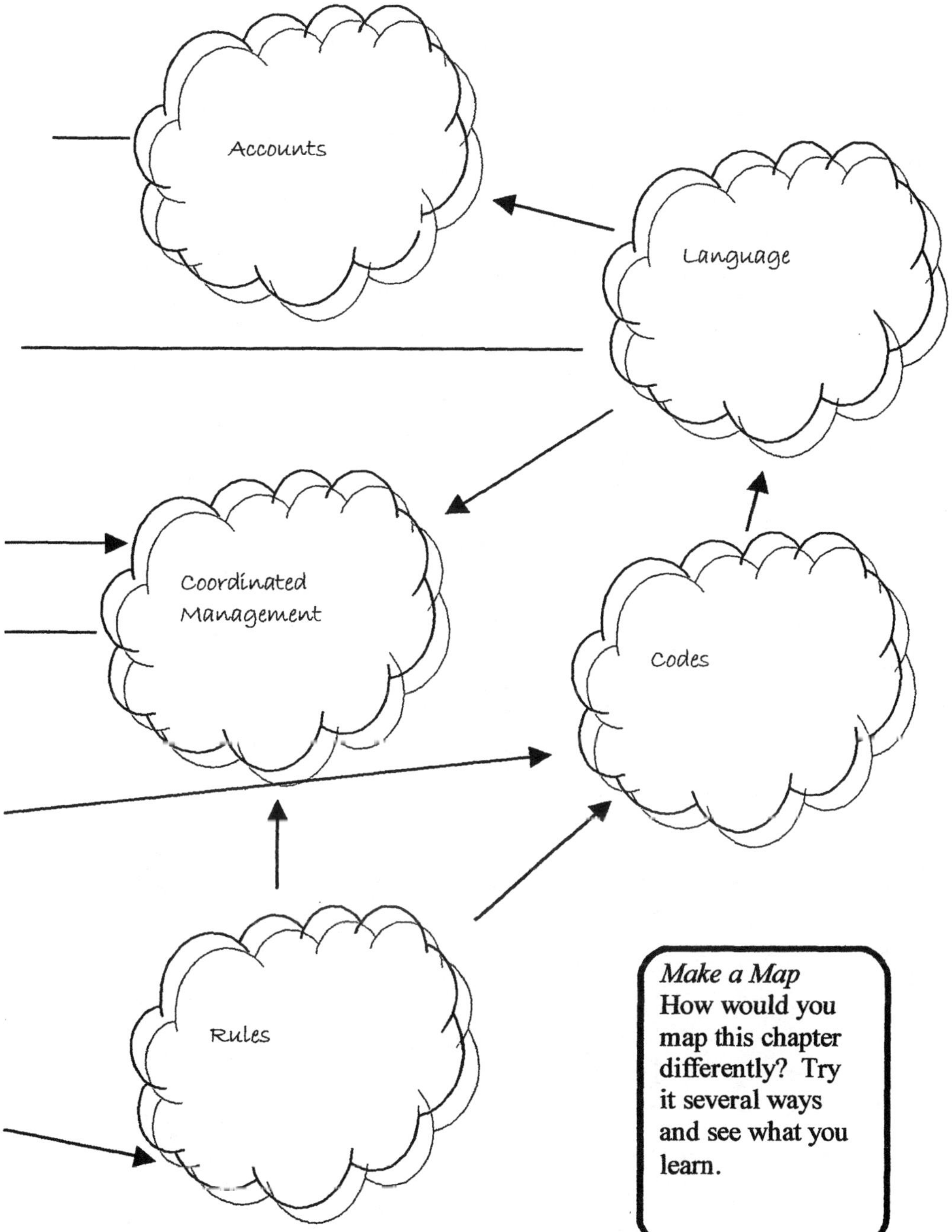

Make a Map
How would you map this chapter differently? Try it several ways and see what you learn.

WORD PUZZLE

Using the clues on the opposite page, fill in the crossed terms below.

Across:

2. Type of force.
4. Private notion of one's personhood.
5. Strange and charmed.
7. Socially constructed.
8. Study of episodes.
10. Sense of personal history.

Down:

1. ____________ perspective.
3. An explanation or justification of behavior.
4. Linguistic relativity.
6. Type of rule.
9. Elaborated and restricted.

Answer:

1. Communication
2. Logical
3. Account
4. Self
5. Loop
6. Regulative
7. Socially constructed
8. Ethogeny
9. Codes
10. Autobiography

CHALLENGES

Internet Challenges

Search for sites on the subject of "Netiquette" and read various guidelines for using the Internet and e-mail. Based on this research and your own experience, how would you answer the following?

1. How is Internet communication a form of coordinated management?

2. What kinds of Internet cultures do you see? How do you explain Internet cultures from the perspective of linguistic relativity?

3. Would you say that e-mail is primarily an elaborated or restricted code, and what are the consequences of this?

Using Your Whole Brain

Think for a few minutes about the language commonly used in your family. What words and phrases are repeated and used within the family? If you need to, listen to family talk and make note of expressions used.

Create a word collage. You can cut words out of magazines or draw letters freehand in colorful artistic ways, or even use a Word Art program on your computer. You are encouraged to have members of your family do this together as a family activity.

What do you learn about your family from the collage? If possible, have family members look at it and talk about what they see there.

THEORY TO ACTION

Interview a good friend about his or her life. Spend an hour or more asking questions about your friend's early experiences, childhood, family, values, philosophy, work, hobbies, and other topics of interest. If possible, tape the conversation so that you can analyze it later. In your interview, what did you notice about the following:

1. Concept of self, especially I_1 and I_2.
2. Agency and autobiography.
3. Emotional syndromes.
4. The constructions arising from accounts.
5. Hierarchies of meaning with special attention to text and context.
6. Elaborated and/or restricted codes.

CASES

My Case: Margaret Oldham*

Margaret Oldham is a highly successful psychotherapist in her thirties. She works hard at what she does, which is to help people and to work on improving her own personal relationships. She is happily and proudly married. She has a well-articulated and mature belief system.

Margaret believes in self-reliance and individual fulfillment. Growing up in the United States, she learned from her parents that the best you can do is to work hard and take pride in your accomplishments. Live up to your own values as best you can. At the same time, she believes that people are very different and tolerance is necessary to build relationships. Relationships require give-and-take. We cannot make great demands on one another, but must be willing to accommodate appropriately when necessary. Ultimately, each person is responsible for his or her life. The best we can hope for in a relationship is clear communication of individual feelings, wants, and needs. We should try to be flexible and willing to tolerate differences, but in the end if another person does not meet our needs, we must move on.

Margaret takes great interest in the diversity among people. She finds difference stimulating, and she enjoys learning from other people's thoughts, ideas, and problems. She does not believe that she can solve other people's problems for them, but she can help them understand their problems so that they can help themselves. Being an adult means accepting personal responsibility. While we get joy and satisfaction from others, in the final analysis, we are alone.

My Analysis: Margaret Oldham's reality is very much like that of many Americans. In the United States, we learn that we are individuals and responsible for our own successes and failures. This view is deeply imbedded in the North American mind. Margaret's theory of personhood is consistent with this cultural ideal that persons are individuals who make choices and decisions affecting their lives. People do have relationships with one another, but relationships consist of the give-and-take between individuals. In Harré's model of personhood, Margaret's view is heavily loaded toward individual realization and active agency. Margaret's theory of self is consistent with this view. She sees herself as a person who has taken control of her life and is living the best she can.

Her view of emotion would also be consistent with this theory. Emotions are personal and individual, and they are to be expressed to others so we all know where we stand with those we care about. The concept of rules is probably not very meaningful to Margaret, but she does admit to certain rules such as being yourself and taking command of your life. She probably does not realize that these rules, like all others, are socially constructed. Because of her emphasis on choice and individual decision making, Margaret's world nicely fits the rule-using approach.

It appears that the self-concept context is very powerful in Margaret's interpretations and actions. She sees herself as a strong and independent person, and her relationships and actions are all understood within this context. Thus she has a charmed loop in which her independent self-image is bolstered by her decisions and choices. She seems moved by a strong practical force, in which she acts to accomplish goals in her life, and a contextual force, in which her self-image provides a logic of meaning and action for all she does.

Margaret seems to speak in an elaborated code. This is natural considering her background, upbringing, and individualistic view of the world. She would oppose a closed-role system, and the open-role system that is most comfortable to her requires thoughtful, elaborated language and personalized appeals.

*This case is elaborated by Robert N. Bellah, et. al., *Habits of the Heart* (Berkeley: University of California Press, 1985), p. 13.

Your Case: "Warrior of God or Terrorist"

Kavosh Dehpanah was born on a small family farm on the plains to the south of the small city of Semnan. Semnan is no more than an oversized walled watering hole 150 miles along the old highway east from Teheran. The city is nestled against the Elburz Mountains whose run-off provides the city's water. From Semnan the barren plateau of Iran stretches for many hundreds of miles over the horizon to the south and east. This is the Dasht-i-kavir Desert, much of which is composed of salt rather than sand. The salt blasts the gray walls of the Dehpanah farm, wearing away the clay stone. Kavosh's family is fortunate because they have a well which provides their water for most of the year. In the driest part of the season they must pay for their water from the local kanat system, an ancient network of deep mountain wells and long tunnels which carry this water to the farms.

Kavosh's family has grown wheat as its main crop for generations. They have also maintained a crop of poppies for opium and an orchard of a few dozen small lime trees. They also maintain a meager flock of sheep and goats. In prosperous years they may have a donkey, cow, or camel to raise for food or extra income.

On the farm, Kavosh's family consists of his parents, his two brothers and two sisters, his grandfather, both of his grandmothers, an aunt and uncle, and two cousins. Kavosh's family, like almost everyone around Sernnan, are Shi'ite Muslims as is 95% of the Iranian population. They follow the Shari'ah (Divine Law) as their guidelines by which to live: They pray to Allah five times a day, pay alms, and fast, and everyone has paid at least one pilgrimage to Mecca, the Holy City of Islam. Their politics define God as the only Legislator, and they believe that their leaders only carry out the laws but do not create them. Shi'ites put their complete faith in the Imam as the sole executor of God's law. The Imam is the ruler of the community and the inheritor of the prophet's teachings. The Imam is the enlightened one. His position has three duties: to rule the Muslim community as the representative of Mohammed, the prophet; to interpret religion, science, politics, and the law to the masses; and to guide men in the spiritual life. Because of the light within him, the Imam's authority goes unquestioned, and his decisions are infallible on spiritual and religious matters.

The Dehpanah family, like most Iranians, characterize themselves as a people in an environment of constant fluid change. They have survived outside invaders from the early Greeks and Romans and the Persians through the crusades; English and Russian colonization; and finally, Western civilization's insatiable quest for oil. They have also survived the unpredictable farming and irrigation conditions inherent in their country as well as a myriad of inept governments. To them, the only stability in their ever changing lives is their historical pride, their religious dedication, and an ancient sense of social hierarchy.

In order to save their country, the Middle East, and Allah's land, the Imam told the people that they must eradicate the devil from the world. Therefore, when Kavosh is sent to a training camp by the ILF, he goes for Allah. He learns to smuggle and detonate explosives and to handle small arms. He becomes a warrior of Allah. His ultimate contribution would be to die for Allah in the struggle to destroy the devil.

His first mission for Allah was to drive a van that assisted in the escape of some more seasoned brothers from Western devils after an attack on an Israeli shopping center. Then the ILF allowed him to participate directly in a coordinated attack on two airports in Greece and Italy. Several of his comrades died for Allah, but he escaped. Next came his ultimate mission; the ILF sent him and three other brothers to southern Europe in order to hijack a jet full of devils. Their plan was discovered before they were ready to take over the plane and they had to act prematurely. The jet was still on the ground, and they had to take fifty-three hostages and issue demands. The jet was quickly surrounded by an assault team of commandos. They were in a stalemate.

Because Kavosh and his comrades believe it an honor to sacrifice themselves as martyrs to Allah, combined with a strong Iranian value of aberu (saving face), there was no backing down, no compromise. Again, there was the dichotomous view of black and white, win or lose, and no in-betweens. They were trapped with no way out. The opposition was not giving in, and they could not give in either. Therefore, they set explosives on the jet and pulled the pins on incendiary grenades.

*Adapted from a student paper written by Rob Hampson, Humboldt State University, Winter, 1986. Reprinted with permission. The case is fictitious.

Your Analysis: In your analysis, consider some of the following issues. In what ways is the world of the "terrorist' socially constructed, and what rules derive from this construction? How is our response to the actions of such individuals socially constructed, and what rules do we use to decide how to respond? Discuss the nature of personhood in the culture of the Dehpanah family. How is this different from your own? Discuss the social construction of emotions in the Shi'ite culture. What contexts and logical forces seem to be operating for the Sh'ite culture as evidenced in this story? Do you detect any charmed or strange loops here?

CRITICAL INCIDENT

The Mediation Center

You administer a community mediation center in which disputes of all types are referred from the local courts and other agencies. You have a staff of trained volunteer mediators who work together in co-mediation teams of two. Typically, a case will involve two disputants and two mediators. Cases include neighbor disputes (such as barking dogs and trash in the yard), consumer problems, landlord-tenant disputes, small claims matters, minor criminal offenses, and others. In mediation, disputants work together with the mediators to settle their differences and come to an agreement, which is usually put in writing.

The mediation center has a good success rate. About 65% of cases reach agreement, and there is a general feeling among mediators that even cases that do not reach a written agreement at least allow disputants to talk to one another and come to a better mutual understanding.

There is serious problem, however. Research has shown that disputes between people of different cultures are hard to resolve. The agreement rate is less in these cases, and since you have a mixed-race community, you get lots of these types of disputes. For example, a Black youth may be involved in a dispute with a Korean shopkeeper, or a White tenant might be involved in a rent dispute with a Black apartment manager.

You decide that your mediators need special training in intercultural disputes. What will be included in this training? Use material from Chapter 9 to design a training program.

NOTES

Communication Theory and Scholarship

Theory in the Proce

System Theory

Theories of Signs a

Theories of Discou

Theories of Messag

Theories of Messag

Theories of Symbo

Theories of Social a

Theories of Experie

Critical Theories

Communication in Relationships

Communication in Group Decision Making

Communication in Organizational Networks

Communication and Media

Chapter 10

Theories of Experience and Interpretation

- What is the role of conscious experience in knowledge?
- How do persons interpret texts?
- How is culture made?
- How can cultures be understood?
- How can communication forms be compared across cultures?

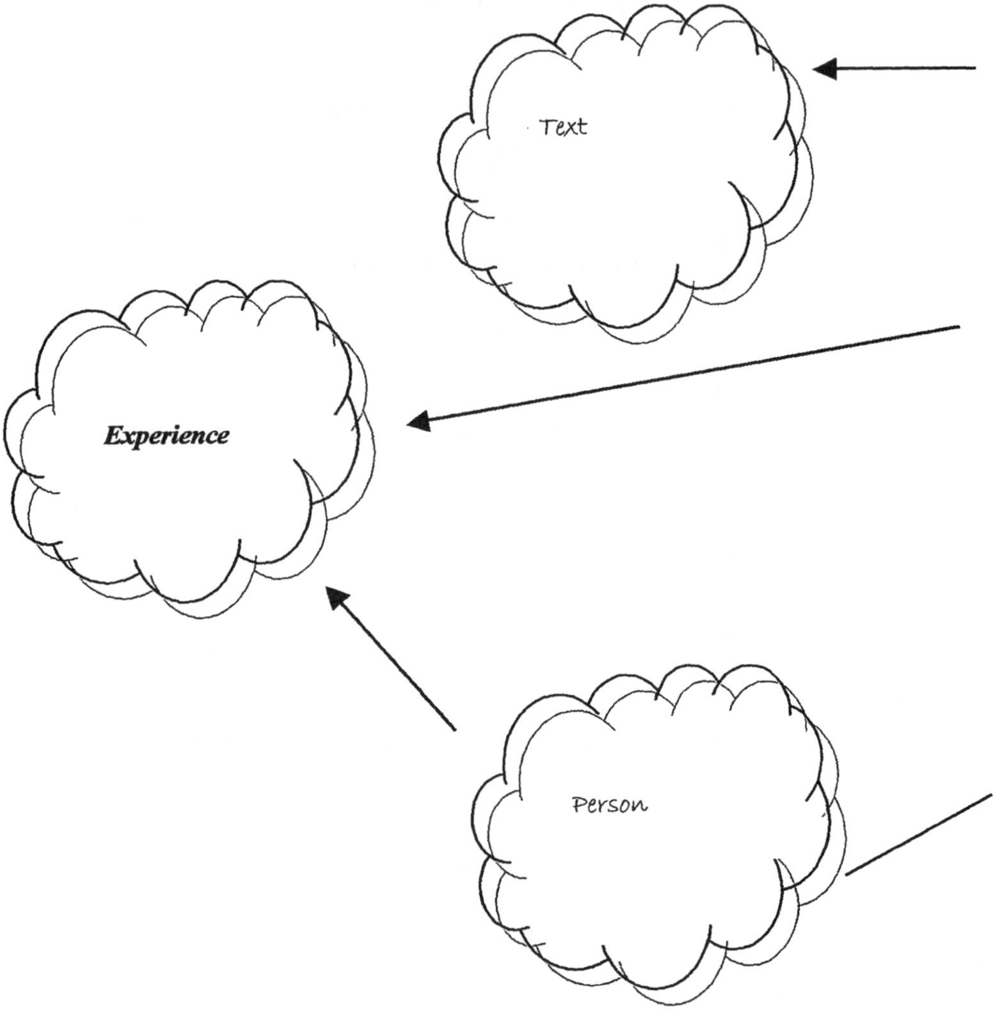

Chapter 10 Map
Theories of Experience and Interpretation

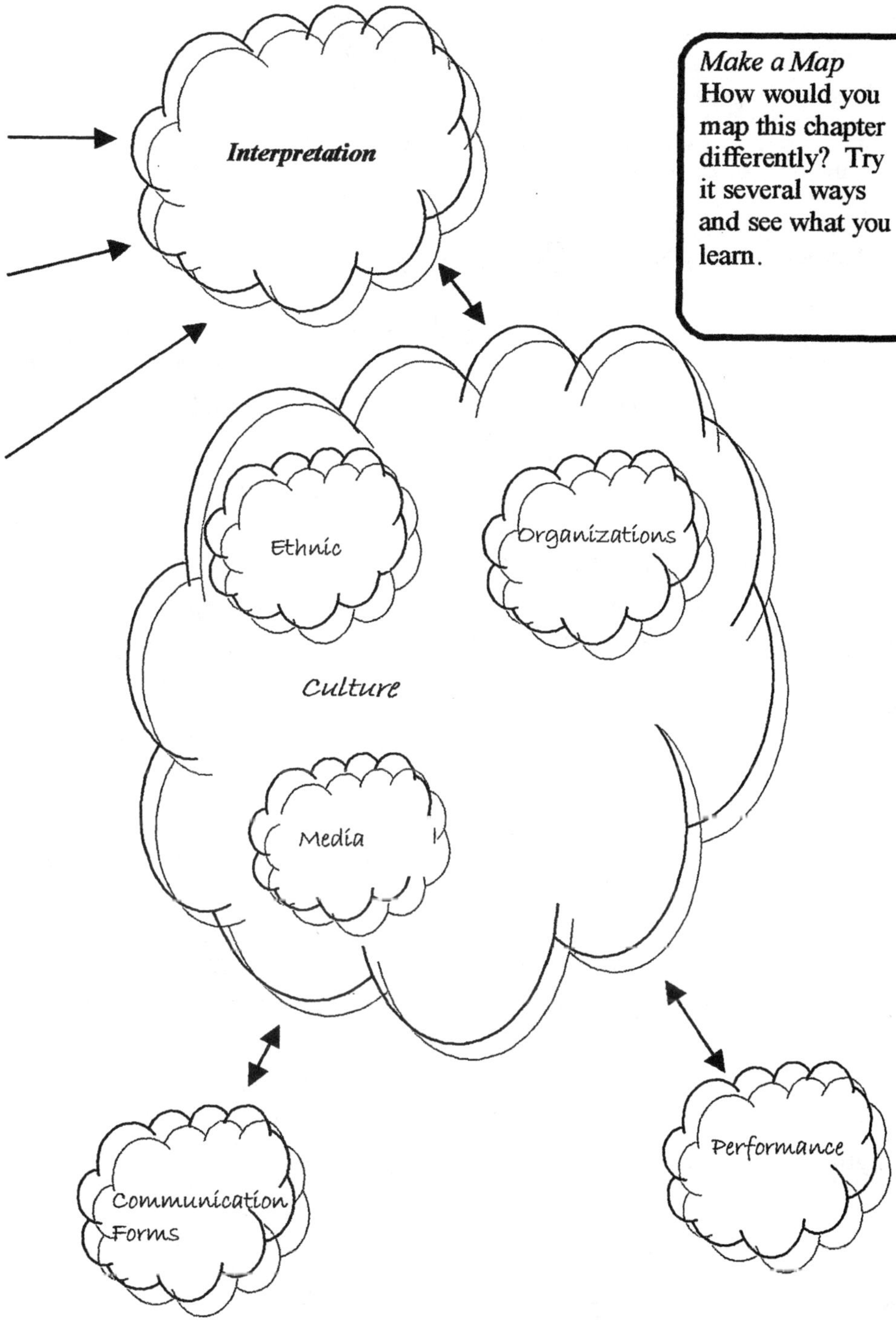

Make a Map
How would you map this chapter differently? Try it several ways and see what you learn.

WORD PUZZLE

Below is a series of phrases from the chapter. Each letter in the phrase has been assigned a numerical code. Using the code, the clue, the free letters, and your knowledge of the chapter, fill in the missing letters.

1. Associated primarily with Heidegger.

H _ _ M _ _ _ _ _ _ _   P H _ _ _ M _ _ _ _ _ _

25 26 22 15 26 19 26 12 1 18 7   4 25 26 19 2 15 26 19 2 24 2 17 20

A B C D E F G H I J K L M N O P Q R S T U V W X Y Z

H = 25, M = 15, P = 4

2. Associated primarily with Stanley Fish.

R _ _ _ _ R   -R _ _ _ _ _ _ _   _ _ _ _ R _

6 15 26 4 15 6   6 15 5 23 20 11 5 15   9 8 15 20 6 13

A B C D E F G H I J K L M N O P Q R S T U V W X Y Z

R = 6

3. A meaningful performance repeated regularly by an entire work group.

_ _ G _ _ _ _ _ _ _ _ _ _ L   _ _ _ _ _ L

7 24 23 4 8 25 26 4 14 25 7 8 4 12   24 25 14 6 4 12

A B C D E F G H I J K L M N O P Q R S T U V W X Y Z

G = 23, L = 12

4. Typical, well-understood ways of doing things.

S _ _ _ _ _   R _ _ _ _ _ S

23 15 9 26 16 1   8 3 9 26 11 3 23

A B C D E F G H I J K L M N O P Q R S T U V W X Y Z

R = 8, S = 23

5. From the natives' point of view.

T _ _ C _   _ _ _ C _ _ _ T _ _ _

5 16 6 8 9   4 24 12 8 1 6 17 5 6 18 14

A	B	C	D	E	F	G	H	I	J	K	L	M	N	O	P	Q	R	S	T	U	V	W	X	Y	Z
		8																	5						

6. Public performances in a cultural community.

S _ _ _ _ _   D _ _ _ _

16 21 14 2 5 12   11 24 5 7 5

A	B	C	D	E	F	G	H	I	J	K	L	M	N	O	P	Q	R	S	T	U	V	W	X	Y	Z
			11															16							

Answers

1. HERMENEUTIC PHENOMENOLOGY
2. READER-RESPONSE THEORY
3. ORGANIZATIONAL RITUAL
4. SOCIAL RECIPES
5. THICK DESCRIPTION
6. SOCIAL DRAMA

CHALLENGES

Internet Challenges

Assume that the Internet is a culture. Conduct an ethnography of communication for this culture. Use Hymes' nine categories and Carbaugh's three types of problems.

Using Your Whole Brain

Spend some time in an art gallery and interpret the paintings you see there. In what ways do you use the hermeneutic circle in your interpreting process? How are paintings treated as texts? Which of the several theories of interpretation in this chapter best explains your process of interpretation?

THEORY TO ACTION

On a note page, make a list of every text you must interpret over a four-hour period. Now sit down for a few minutes and reflect on these texts. After reflecting, write answers to the following questions:

1. What elements of the texts themselves provided clues of meaning?

2. What aspects of your own experience provided a basis for interpretation?

3. To what extent were your interpretations culturally determined? Provide a thick description of your meanings and uses of the texts from a cultural point of view.

4. Were any of the texts performances? Describe these and your interpretations.

5. Were any of the texts mediated? How were your interpretations shaped by the interpretive community of which you are a member?

CASES

My Case: Donahue

"Donahue" was one of the oldest and most popular television talk shows. Each weekday Donahue discussed a theme, and he usually had one or more expert guests, lay guests, and an audience. The guests were usually invited to make statements, and then Donahue walked around the audience fielding questions and comments. The show often dealt with controversial issues such as nurses hooked on drugs, anger clinics, and sex among the old. The tone of the program was usually spirited, and the show seemed to thrive on controversy and emotion.

Donahue originally broadcast from Chicago, but moved to New York in the late 1980s. He sometimes took the show on the road to broadcast from various locations around the country.

My Analysis: The Donahue Show could be analyzed in a number of ways using the material in this chapter. For example, I could do a phenomenological analysis. This could be done for one of three purposes. First, I might want to determine what constitutes the Donahue format. Here we would bracket our experience and concentrate on our experience of the program. Second, I might want to experience people's statements about various issues. Again, we would listen carefully in a reflective attitude to what people say on the program. Third, I might be interested in how audiences themselves experience the program. Here we would interview viewers and conduct a phenomenological reduction on what they say.

In any case, language would be vitally important in any phenomenological study we might want to conduct. What categories of meaning and experience are suggested by what people say on the program and what they say about it? In the social phenomenology tradition, we would acknowledge our own experiences and meanings and the ways in which these color our analysis of the program or its audience.

Any analysis we would conduct on Donahue from the perspective of this chapter would involve interpretation in one form or another. Several approaches are possible. For example, we could examine tapes or transcripts of old Donahue shows and conduct textual interpretation on them. We could use Donahue as a reflection of certain cultural ways of thinking and conduct an ethnography based on the program. Or we could interview various people who regularly watched the program in an attempt to describe a variety of interpretive media communities.

Here we will borrow from Donal Carbaugh, who has done an extensive ethnography of the Donahue program after viewing and reviewing numerous Donahue programs.* His analysis involves much interpretation of textual material, so it illustrates text hermeneutics as well. Because Carbaugh explictly uses his own cultural knowledge and reads extensively about American culture, his analysis is very much in the tradition of hermeneutic phenomenology. He uses Donahue as a case of American culture, and he uses the program to show how many Americans think about communication. The categories of culture uncovered in this analysis are not universal in the United States, but they do seem to apply to many citizens.

Carbaugh says that Donahue reflected certain aspects of American culture and provideed a forum in which people could "talk American." Three categories of meaning (typifications in Schutz's theory) are predominant in the Donahue text and in the American culture as well. These are the individual, choice, and self. People are considered to be individuals with personal rights guaranteed by 'the system." Americans not only value individual rights, but consider them as political guarantees. For example, on one program a couple said that a doctor had disconnected their son from his life support system because the son had been declared brain dead. This was viewed as a violation of the parents' individual rights, and some audience members seemed more alarmed about this violation of rights than about the fate of the son.

Because of their emphasis on the individual, it is not surprising that Americans treat the self as distinct from other selves. They treat themselves as objects to be discussed and described. Carbaugh found that spokespersons on Donahue tend to reject traditional roles in favor of personal choice. Roles prescribe, and Americans are impatient with categories that suggest how they should behave. People are free to choose from a vast array of alternatives in their lives, and they do so voluntarily. For example, one show featured a "triad," three people who claimed to be married to one another. In this arrangement any member of the "marriage" could have sex with any other member, and they permitted sexual relations outside the arrangement as well. They defended this strange situation on the basis of personal choice.

The speech event in this culture is defined as "communication." When people talk in certain desired ways, they are "communicating." This communication consists of two acts, being honest and sharing. If one is really communicating, one must "be honest" above all. You can commit a variety of errors and sins, but all is forgiven if you are honest about it. For example, one nurse described how she had stolen patients' pain medication to support her drug habit. The audience was appalled, but praised her for being honest.

Second, communication involves sharing, or telling about yourself and listening to other people do the same. Genuine communication can't occur if people are unwilling to share their feelings. In this culture, then, "communication" is seen as a process in which individuals share with one another through talk.

What does this form of communication require? It requires that (a) people must be open, (b) they must be supportive, and (c) they must be flexible. So good communication occurs when people are willing to hear others being honest, when they support the individuality of the other person, and when they allow others to be who they are.

*From Donal Carbaugh, *Talking American: Cultural Discourses on Donahue* (Norwood, NJ: Ablex Publishing, 1988).

Your Case: "I don't watch T.V."*

Fred: No, I don't watch television. I never owned a T.V. and never lived in a house with one. Oh, actually we did have one when I was a kid, but I only watched it a few hours a week. It wasn't that we weren't allowed to; I just didn't want to. T.V. does draw you in. I know when I'm around a T.V., it's hard to tear myself away. I like the moving colors. For me, it's like going to a foreign country. It shows a little life we'll never see—Vietnam, politicians, shoot-em up. It's not real. My non-viewing rarely comes up in conversations. My friends find it hilarious, though, that if I'm house-sitting, I might spend the whole day watching T.V. I have to admit I sometimes don't know what's going on with world events. I think watching T.V. is like an addiction. Perhaps I'm like an alcoholic who remains that and knows he can't take a drink. I know I'd be an addict, so I just refrain. I was really involved with music as a teenager, and I wouldn't want that to happen again to such excess. Actually, I almost bought a television yesterday. I wanted to have one around, but I decided against it because I didn't want to watch it in excess. Am I different from other people? Yeah, I'm more introspective. I can entertain myself more easily. I read a lot and talk on the phone a lot. I'm intellectually oriented, and people notice this. T.V. makes some people ill physically—which may be a factor in my decision not to have one. You avoid things that aren't good for you. I have a tenant, for, example, who hears a high frequency when she uses a computer, so she can't have anything to do with computers. I may subconsciously know this about T.V. and avoid it for that reason. A lot of T.V. is sick—a lot of the programming. A lot of the news is not in good taste; it is sensational and not factual or truthful.

Patty: I grew up watching T.V. I was born in 1950, very much the T.V. generation. I grew up on Saturday cartoons; they were very much part of my history. I had a T.V. until about six months ago. I watched in the evenings, then started watching the "Today" show, and even started coming home at lunch to watch a soap opera. Finally, my boyfriend and I decided to sell the T.V. Cable cost too much, and we needed the space for the bird cage. It's been great. We play with the birds, read more, talk more, listen to music, make love more. We spend more time together, and it's more pleasant. People are really curious about why we don't have a T.V. My friend's mother thinks we're really deprived. Occasionally, we get together with other people to watch "Twin Peaks," but for me it's the social aspect that's important, not the show. Basically, people can't relate to not having a T.V. T.V. is the center of so many lives. They ask, "What do you do?" I say, "Back in our grandparents' day, people used to do this thing called 'talking.'" I listen to tapes and records; I listen to the radio. Occasionally we have people over just to talk. T.V. is like alcohol. Everybody does it; it's expected. Yet alcohol became an interference in my life. The same was true of T.V. Both were substitutes for more meaningful pursuits. If they were simply alternatives, that would be fine. But both tend to take on a negative role. I phased out alcohol—it was more and more of an intrusion; same with T.V.—when it was off, I did more positive things.

***Constructed from unpublished research data provided by Karen Foss, 1991. See Karen A. Foss & Alison Alexander, "Exploring the Margins of Television Viewing," *Communication Reports*, 9 (Winter, 1996): 61-68.**

Your Analysis: What do these excerpts tell you about a particular media culture? Conduct a textual interpretation of them to determine what meanings are revealed. How might interviews such as these be used as part of an ethnography of communication? What do you learn about a particular interpretive media culture from statements such as these?

CRITICAL INCIDENT

Working Abroad

You have received a wonderful opportunity to work for a year as a teacher of English in Japan. You will be working for a private school specializing in training businessmen (literally men). Your job is to teach them English and American culture.

You are really quite excited about this opportunity. There is just one problem. You know no Japanese and very little about Japanese culture. Your company offers no training, and you will be "thrown in" without any special preparation. You just have your wits and college education to serve you.

How will you proceed? What will you do? How can Chapter 10 help you?

Communication Theory and Scholarship

Theory in the Proce

System Theory

Theories of Signs a

Theories of Discou

Theories of Messag

Theories of Messag

Theories of Symbo

Theories of Social and Cultural Reality

Theories of Experience and Interpretation

Critical Theories

Communication in Relationships

Communication in Group Decision Making

Communication in Organizational Networks

Communication and Media

Chapter 11

Critical Theories

- How is social power enacted in discourse?
- How are culture and ideology determined?
- How is gender determined?
- Why does gender matter?

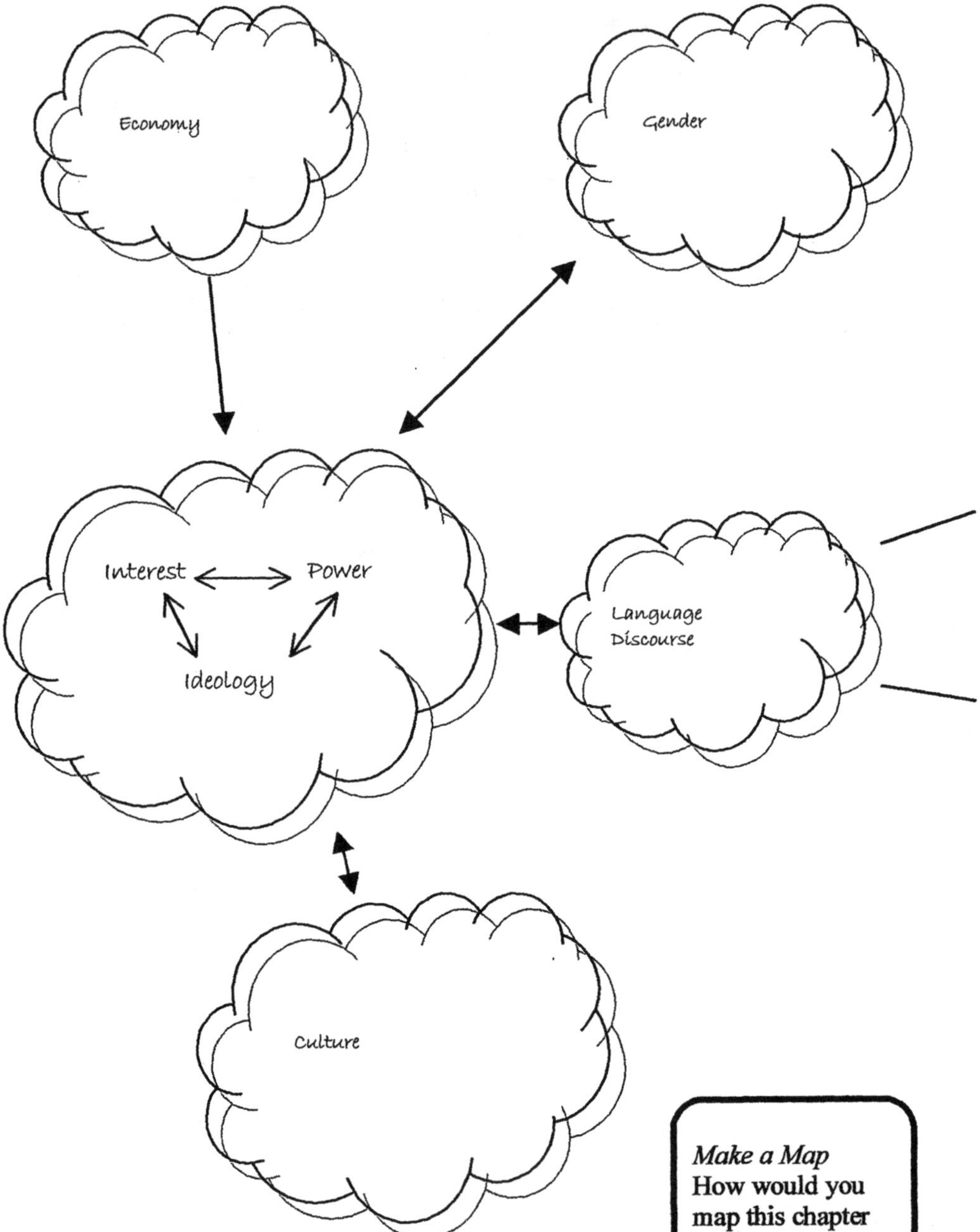

Make a Map
How would you map this chapter differently? Try it several ways and see what you learn.

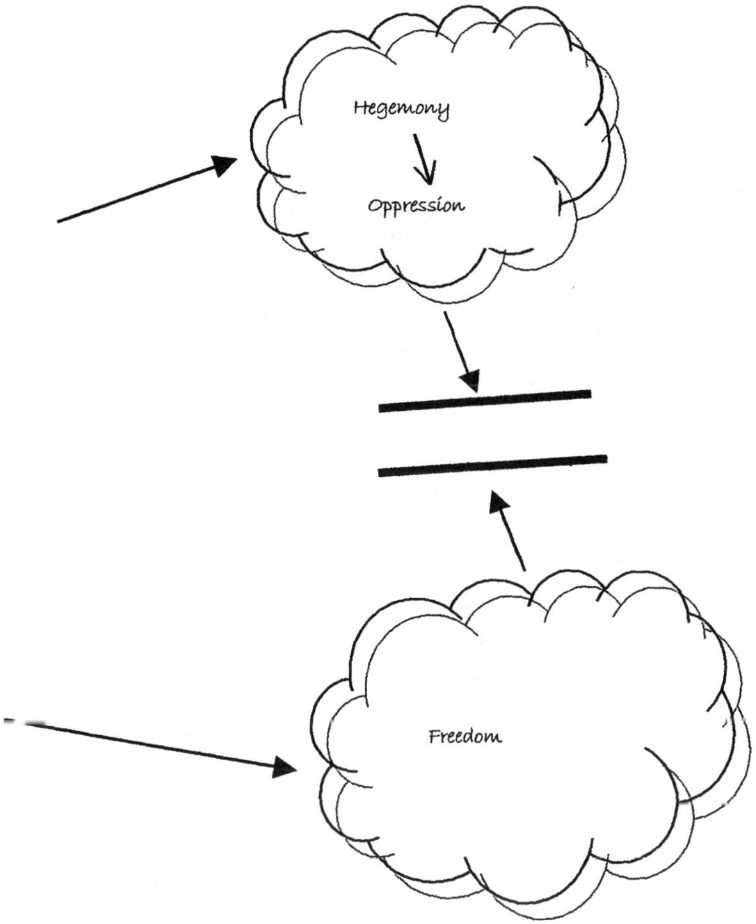

Chapter 11 Map
Critical Theories

WORD PUZZLE

In each space below, fill in the correct term from the chapter. Next to each line is a clue. All of the letters for each column are listed below the column, but in mixed-up order. Use these as a further clue to the correct words.

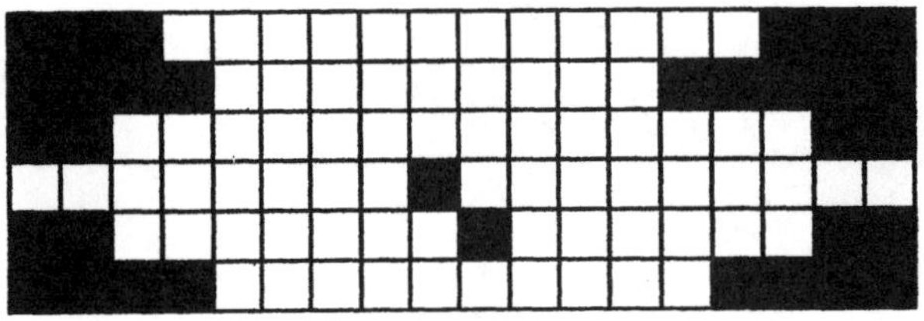

1. *Involving international media*
2. *Important force in hegemony*
3. *Many causes*
4. *Way of thinking; 5. School of thought*
6. *A production; 7. A basis of oppression*
8. *A new way of talking*

I O T E   O A I

L I V C T L R M I A

U O T U R O E R S N N E

C O D S S I T U R N E D L D

E P L N D Y E F G E N K E R

I D O V E R G C O A T I O N F U R T

NOTES

Answers:

1. Postcolonial
2. Discourse
3. Overdetermined
4. Ideology
5. Frankfurt
6. Culture
7. Gender
8. Invitation

CHALLENGES

Internet Challenges

1. What's been going on in the Frankfurt School lately? Find out on the Internet.

2. What's been going on in the Centre for Contemporary Cultural Studies lately? Use the Internet to find out.

3. Find six sites on feminism, three that are generally favorable and three that are generally negative. On what points are they divided?

Using Your Whole Brain

1. Leaf through several popular magazines looking at advertisements. Don't be critical; just react intuitively and emotionally. What catches your eye? What appeals to you?

2. Now analyze the ads more systematically from a critical studies point of view. What forces of hegemony seem to be apparent? What interests are being promoted? What kind of culture is being produced?

3. Now leaf through the same magazine advertisements again, putting your analysis aside. What new intuitions and emotions now govern your impressions?

THEORY TO ACTION

Critical theory has been the basis for much activism during the past century. Study the life and work of one of the following activists or an activist of your choice.

- Che Guevara
- Harvey Milk
- Gloria Steinem
- Saul Alinsky
- Angela Davis
- Stokely Carmichael
- Abbie Hoffman
- Winona LaDuke
- Ralph Nader
- Emma Goldman

CASES

My Case: "Dreamworlds"

"Dreamworlds" is a documentary film on the treatment of women in rock videos, produced by Sut Jhally, a professor at the University of Massachusetts. The film is a remarkable exposition of the use of visual images in rock videos, focusing on the place of female images in these productions. The thesis is that rock videos tend to tap into an adolescent male fantasy of women as objects of sex play, to be viewed and manipulated sexually.

My Analysis: "Dreamworlds" shows that rock videos, like all media events, are cultural productions in which certain meanings are reproduced and accentuated. Specifically, in addition to whatever else may be produced in these videos, they tend to use female images in a sexual, objectified way. Producers do not intend to demean women, but the images they employ, in reflecting and reproducing certain deep cultural values, certainly do so. The interests of men are served at the expense of those of women. Thus a segment of a powerful ideology is reproduced in these films, and a clear case of hegemony results.

This film is produced in the cultural-studies tradition, and it shows how the media can be powerful in promoting certain cultural images over other ones. The struggle, or conflict, in society at large is that of woman as competent person versus woman as object. In showing how rock videos promote one side in this clash over the other, the film also illustrates the radical feminist agenda. Here we see that the objectification of women is deeply embedded in productions that serve male interests. The film also shows how this view is articulated and reflective of meanings seen in a wide variety of sources, not just rock videos.

Many men and women adopt the meaning of woman as sex object and play out this fantasy in their material practices in everyday life. The gang rape scene from the feature film *The Accused*, shown in juxtaposition with scenes from various rock videos, persuasively illustrates this articulation.

"Dreamworlds" presents an oppositional reading, exposing meanings in rock videos that are not intended by their producers and may not necessarily be obvious to viewers. Such viewers may well become co-opted into the worldview depicted in these videos. As a critical piece, then, "Dreamworlds" has the potential of emancipation because it makes us aware of a certain form of oppression. This kind of work builds power for marginalized groups through the promotion of self-reflection. Only when society is free to explore the meanings of cultural productions in these ways will a truly ideal speech situation be possible.

Your Case and Analysis: Your Favorite Sitcom

After reading Chapter 11, watch an episode or two or your favorite television sitcom with a new eye. (If you do not have a favorite sitcom, choose any such program for this assignment.) How would a critical theorist view this program? Can you give the show a feminist reading? In what ways is it a cultural production, and how does it contribute to hegemony?

CRITICAL INCIDENT

The Advertising Agency

You have just graduated from college and have landed a very nice job in your field: communication specialist for an advertising agency. This is a great job for you because this agency concentrates on fashion, one of your main interests. The company specializes in magazine ad layouts and has contracts with several major design houses. Agency advertisements have been placed in numerous major American and European magazines.

As communication specialist, you are expected to know about persuasion and the "psychology" of influence. You do know about these things, but you know more. You realize that advertisements are cultural productions, and they always have important effects beyond selling a product.

How will you use this broader knowledge in your job? How will it affect what you do and how you work as a member of the team? You expect to grow with the job and move up in the company. Use Chapter 11 to formulate a philosophy to guide your work in this career.

Communication Theory and Scholarship

Theory in the Proce

System Theory

Theories of Signs a

Theories of Discou

Theories of Messag

Theories of Messag

Theories of Symbo

Theories of Social a

Theories of Experie

Critical Theories

Communication in

Communication in

Communication in Organizational Networks

Communication and Media

Chapter 12

Communication in Relationships

- How are relationships established, defined, maintained, and changed through communication?
- What forms of communication affect relationships, and how do these communication forms work?
- What are the types of relational patterns, and how is communication different in these various forms?
- What aspects of relationships are managed in communication, and how do communicators manage these challenges?

Make a Map
How would you map this chapter differently? Try it several ways and see what you learn.

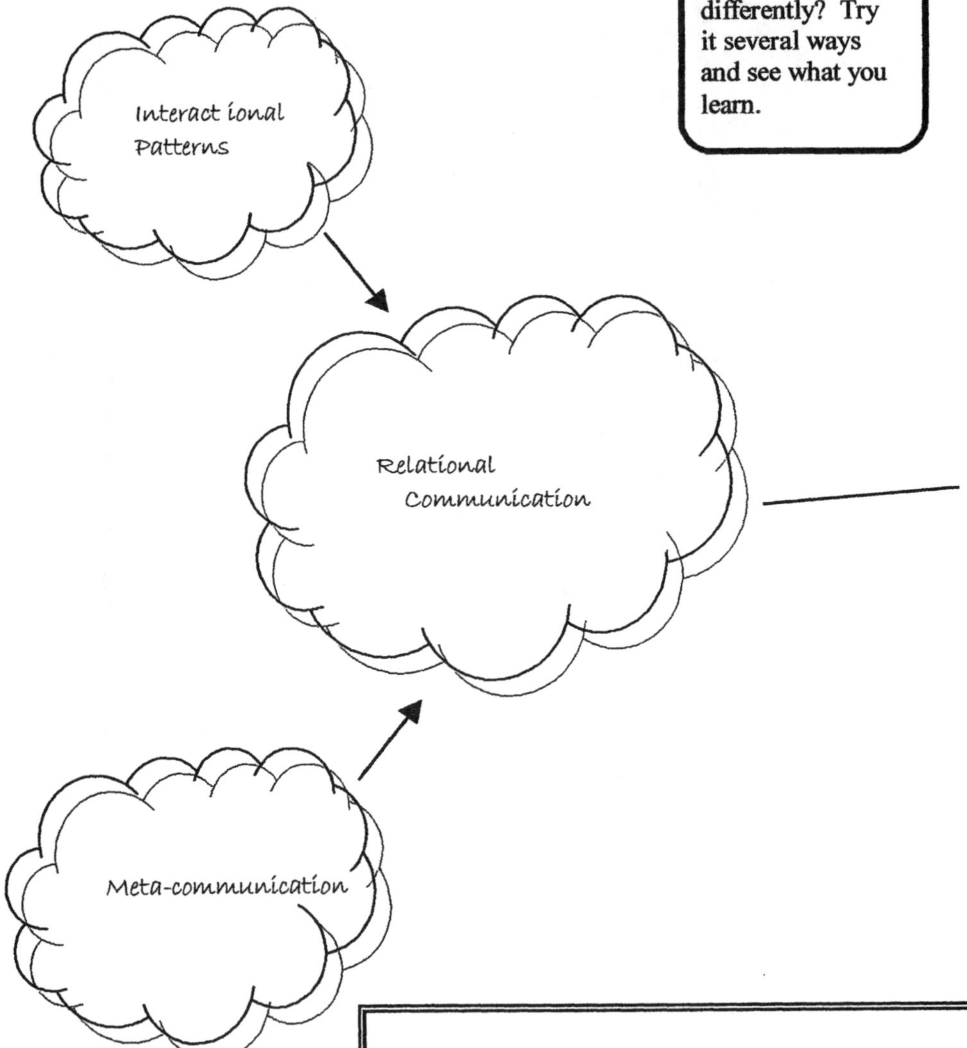

Chapter 12 Map
Communication in Relationships

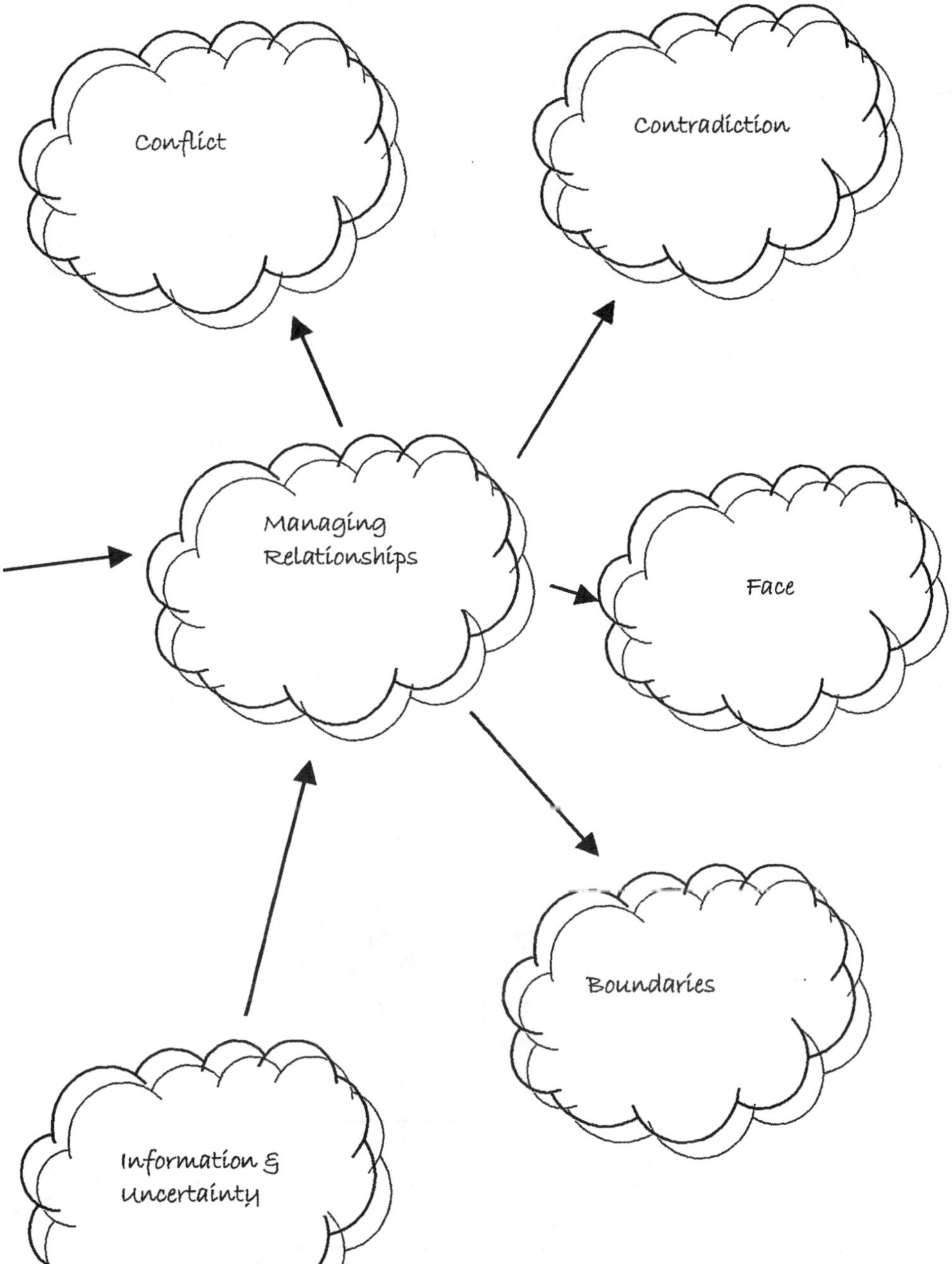
Conflict
Contradiction
Managing Relationships
Face
Boundaries
Information & Uncertainty

WORD PUZZLE

Below is a series of quotations from the chapter. Place the correct letter combinations in the tiles to unscramble the definition. A dash represents a space.

Example:

OVE   I-L   U.-   -YO

I-L	OVE	-YO	U.-

1.

COM	S-E	-BE	N-O	AVO	TIO	N.-
T,-	IDA	MUN	MUN	OY-	TIO	IOR
ICA	NCE	NO-	R,-	IRE	CT-	IND
BES	COM	ICA	AT-	MPL	HAV	

2.

RE-	IAL	-SY	ENT	-MO	F-A	ENS
IS-	A-D	DIC	TOR	EN-	IC-	TWE
S-O	TWO	TRA	STE	-OR	A-T	Y-E
ECT	M.-	ION	CON	LEM	-BE	

3.

E-R	SEN	TO-	OTH	F-I	.--	OF-
PRE	HE-	MAG	FAC	ONE	E-I	N-T
CE-	EFE	RS-	ERS	'S-	SEL	

4.

ELA	ASI	TIO	NET	ION	INT	CY-
-TH	ND-	IP.	-IS	NSH	E-A	-PE
-IN	SOC	-OF	A-R	SUR	NG-	-IN
RAT	DIS	ESS	IAL	CLO	CRE	IMA
ROC	E-P					

5.

T-N	NNO	-CA	TE.	OT-	ONE	MUN
ICA	COM					

Answers:

1. AVO IDA NCE -BE HAV IOR S-E MPL
OY- NO- COM MUN ICA TIO N-O R,-
AT- BES T,- IND IRE CT- COM MUN
ICA TIO N.-

2. A-D IAL ECT IC- IS- A-T ENS ION
-BE TWE EN- TWO -OR -MO RE- CON
TRA DIC TOR Y-E LEM ENT S-O F-A -
SY STE M.-

3. FAC E-R EFE RS- TO- ONE 'S- SEL
F-I MAG E-I N-T HE- PRE SEN CE-
OF- OTH ERS .--

4. SOC IAL -PE NET RAT ION -IS -TH
E-P ROC ESS -OF -IN CRE ASI NG-
DIS CLO SUR E-A ND- INT IMA CY-
IN- A-R ELA TIO NSH IP.

5. ONE -CA NNO T-N OT- COM MUN ICA
TE.

CHALLENGES

Internet Challenges

1. How are the various functions of relational communication accomplished in e-mail?

2. How is the management of friendship different on the Internet?

3. It is said that "one cannot not communicate." Is this true in e-mail? Why or why not?

4. Do a search for "online dispute resolution." What do you find? Peruse some of these sites and apply relational communication to what happens there.

Using Your Whole Brain

Go through a picture album and pause to study photos of your friends and family. What feelings do you get from each picture? As you look at each picture, do a word association, jotting down all the words that come to mind. If you are artistic, do a bit of free-form sketching to capture some of your feelings about certain pictures. Later, go back and look at your word associations and sketches and see what they tell you about your relationships with these people. Relate your insights to the concepts in the chapter.

THEORY TO ACTION

Interview three friends about relationships that are important to them. In your interviews, try to gain insights about the following dimensions of your friends' relationships:

- Complementarity and Symmetry
- Control patterns
- Contradiction
- Uncertainty reduction
- Face behavior
- Self disclosure, intimacy, and boundary management
- Conflict

CASES

My Case: *Thelma and Louise*

Thelma and Louise was a popular motion picture released in 1991. It is the story of two friends, played by Geena Davis and Susan Sarandon, who go off on a fishing trip together and get more than they bargained for. The first night out, Thelma (Davis) is raped, and Louise (Sarandon) shoots the rapist. The two run from the scene and disable a police car, blow up a truck, and make their way toward the Mexican border in an attempt to escape the policy as well as Thelma's angry husband. This is a film about friendship and relational communication.

My Analysis: Thelma and Louise are friends and have had an ongoing relationship prior to the beginning of the story. Consequently, they do have some idea of what to expect from one another. They have not encountered the situations depicted in the story, however, so new rules and expectations are constantly being negotiated throughout the film. In an early scene, for example, Thelma wants to stay a while at a bar to drink and dance, but Louise is eager to get on the road so that they can reach their fishing destination that evening. They argue about this, but in the end decide to stay.

Over the course of the story, increasing trust builds between the friends, even though Thelma loses Louise's money, which they badly need to get out of the country. This trust building is a good example of metacommunication and the assumption on the part of both characters that each wants to get out of the bad situation in which they have found themselves and that each wants to be loyal to the other. Throughout the film they talk, argue, and persuade one another, and at each juncture, they perceive increasing loyalty in their respective behaviors.

During the time they are together, the relationship increases in intimacy. For example, Thelma learns from Louise's behavior and disclosures that she has had her own experience with rape, which explains why she reacted so aggressively and angrily when she caught a cowboy raping Thelma in the parking lot of the bar. The boundaries between the friends become increasingly fluid as more and more gets revealed.

At the beginning of the story, Thelma and Louise are operating at an orientation level. As they get into various predicaments, they explore affective exchange, and by the end of the drama, they have come to know one another very well indeed and are operating at the level of stable exchange. There seems to be little if anything they are willing to hide from one another. The social penetration process is accelerated between the friends because of the rapidity of the events they face together in their days on the road.

Their interactions are marked by numerous control moves. Because the couple has to make a number of decisions very rapidly, they do attempt to influence one another. In the beginning Louise is clearly dominant. She plans the fishing trip to celebrate her birthday and essentially goads Thelma into getting away from her domineering husband for the weekend. For the most part, Thelma accepts Louise's control moves, but there are exceptions, as when Thelma rejects Louise's decision to leave the bar after one drink. Later, as their relationship develops the control pattern becomes very flexible, as control moves back and forth between the two.

As friends, Thelma and Louise must manage a number of dialectical tensions in their relationship. At the beginning of the story, they are relatively independent from one another. As they get into increasing trouble, however, they find it necessary to depend on one another to meet a variety of needs.

The relationship runs the gamut between affection and instrumentality. It is clear that in the beginning the relationship is strictly one of affection between the two, but as they encounter problems, they must rely on one another to get things done. At the end of the film, it is clear that the relationship has returned to affection and loyalty.

Finally, they also must manage the dialectic of judgment versus acceptance. Throughout the film, the two characters make judgments about one another, and they worry that one of them will make a mistake that gets them caught. Indeed, each does make errors, and the other one lets her know that she did the wrong thing. But once they get coordinated, they develop a degree of confidence and trust, and in the end they are completely accepting of one another and of their joint decisions.

Thelma and Louise's management of the dialectic of expressiveness and protectiveness is especially interesting. While they seemed to swing back and forth between the contradictions on the other dialectics, they managed both poles of this one simultaneously. Throughout the story, they blend and combine expressiveness and protectiveness in almost all of their statements to one another. This is possible because within the situations in which they find themselves they are able to protect one another by expressing their feelings.

There is naturally some conflict between Thelma and Louise, but they generally manage it very well. They are not quick to attribute blame, and they try to come up with cooperative solutions to most of the problems they encounter. For example, at one point Thelma begins talking to a stranger at a gas station. He asks for a ride, but Louise is unwilling to give him one. Thelma and Louise argue about this, and Louise agrees to take him along. This gives Thelma a chance to be with her new friend, and it meets Louise's need to get back on the road.

Thelma and Louise is an excellent case study and illustrates many of the concepts in this chapter very well.

Your Case and Analysis: *Legally Blond*

Rent and view the film *Legally Blond.* Analyze the relationship among the characters in terms of the concepts in this chapter.

CRITICAL INCIDENT

The Silence

You and your spouse have been married for six years. In all, you would say that you have a good marriage. Both of you have college degrees and are pursuing separate careers. You do not have children yet, but are looking forward to a family sometime in the future. So far neither of you has pressed the issue.

You and your spouse are both quite busy. You each work at least 40 hours per week and often more. It is not uncommon for you to bring work home evenings and weekends, and both of you have set up small work areas in separate rooms. Still, you enjoy one another very much and spend time doing fun things together, including movies, going to restaurants, and skiing. You also have some separate interests. You read a lot more than your spouse, and your spouse loves golfing, which you can't stand. You each have friends of your own and quite a few "couple" friends as well. You don't always enjoy or like one another's friends, but that seems to be okay. All in all, you would say that you have a yours-mine-and-ours kind of marriage.

Lately, you have been somewhat irritable, probably because of a lot of stress you are having at work. You know that you are a little hard to live with, but your spouse hasn't said anything about it. You think you should bring the subject up, just to reassure your partner and to explain what you have been going through at work, but you are not quite sure what the reaction will be. So you decide to bring the subject up somewhat tentatively to test the waters.

After breakfast one Saturday morning, you say, "Well, things are a little tense lately, huh?"

"What do you mean?"

"Oh, I'm just feeling, uh, a little strange lately."

"Well, don't worry about it."

You are not sure how to interpret this response. That Saturday, though nothing more is said, things seem a little strained.

You hope your spouse will bring the topic up again, and you wait for this to happen, but it does not. An entire week goes by, and nothing more is said. In fact, your spouse is really quiet all week. You really want to talk about your job situation, but at the same time, you don't really want to rock the boat.

In the following few weeks, your mood doesn't improve much, and your spouse continues to be quiet. Conversation seems hard for some reason.

What do you think you will do? Explain your plan in terms of concepts from Chapter 12.

NOTES

Communication Theory and Scholarship

Theory in the Proce

System Theory

Theories of Signs a

Theories of Discou

Theories of Messag

Theories of Messag

Theories of Symbo

Theories of Social a

Theories of Experience and Interpretation

Critical Theories

Communication in Relationships

Communication in Group Decision Making

Communication in Organizational Networks

Communication and Media

Chapter 13

Communication in Group Decision Making

- **In what ways do the interpersonal and task work of groups affect one another?**
- **What factors enhance and inhibit group success?**
- **How do groups make decisions and solve problems?**

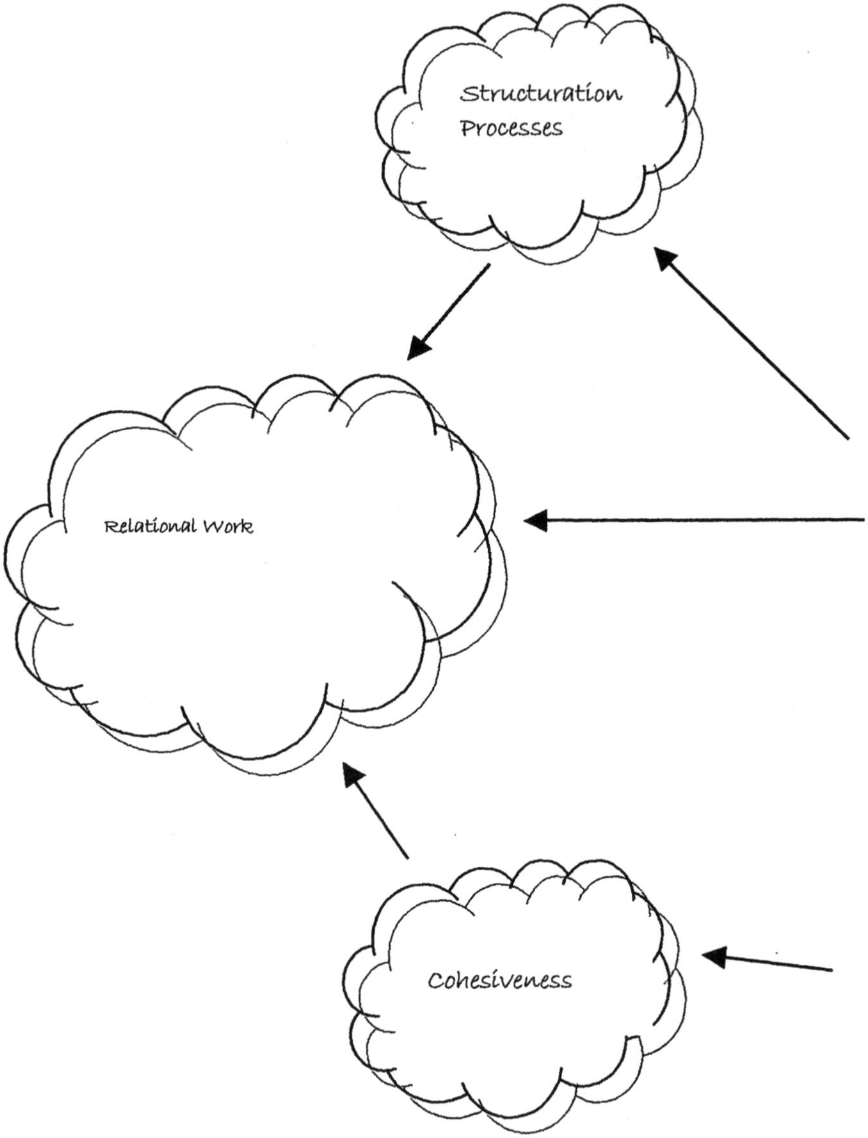

Chapter 13 Map
Communication in Group Decision Making

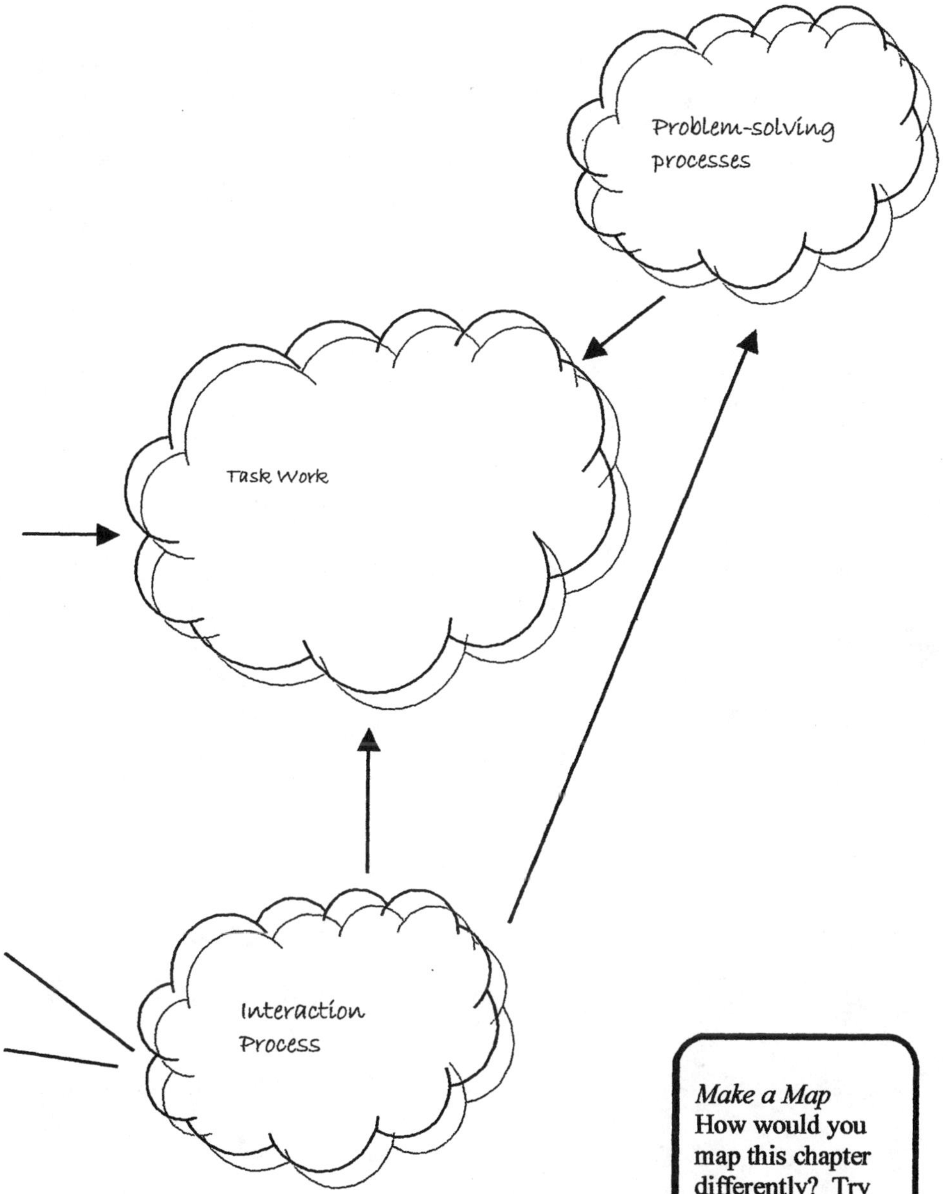

Make a Map
How would you map this chapter differently? Try it several ways and see what you learn.

WORD PUZZLE

On the next page is a list of clues for terms from the chapter. From the clue, figure out the term and find it in the puzzle below. The word may run horizontally, down, up, or diagonally. When you have identified a term, mark it with a magic marker or highlighter. After all the terms are found, look for the hidden message between the words, and write it in the space provided.

S	G	D	R	O	U	P	D	E	C	I	S	I	O	N
M	T	A	R	K	I	N	G	I	S	A	P	R	O	C
E	S	R	S	A	I	N	W	H	I	C	H	G	S	R
O	U	P	U	M	M	E	M	B	E	R	S	S	A	T
T	E	M	P	C	T	A	T	O	A	C	E	H	I	E
V	G	E	C	O	T	N	T	V	E	N	R	G	E	N
C	E	R	O	N	A	U	F	I	E	I	N	A	Y	L
D	E	C	O	I	S	I	R	V	Z	O	N	A	G	N
D	I	N	S	U	O	D	I	A	O	I	I	N	R	G
S	T	R	U	C	P	S	T	T	T	U	N	R	E	E
T	H	E	I	R	E	T	C	S	O	I	C	G	N	I
A	L	S	Y	H	S	E	H	T	E	M	O	F	Y	G
U	Q	I	O	L	F	U	W	I	B	D	C	N	S	M
Q	T	C	I	F	J	U	B	Z	N	T	V	S	B	R
A	S	S	E	M	B	L	Y	Y	A	K	K	B	R	N

Clues:

1. Accumulated effort of group members.
2. "We" feeling.
3. Telling stories.
4. Outcome.
5. Error due to cohesiveness
6. Creating structure.
7. Overall group effort, or energy devoted to task and relationship.

Hidden Message:

Terms:

1. Assembly
2. Cohesiveness
3. Dramatizing
4. Effect
5. Groupthink
6. Structuration
7. Synergy

Hidden Message:

Group decision making is a process in which group members attempt to achieve convergence on a final decision and in so doing structure their social system.

CHALLENGES

Internet Challenges

Virtual conferencing is becoming increasingly popular. Search the Internet for sites on this tool. As you learn more about Internet meetings, think about how the dynamics of groups change as they move from physical space to virtual space. As broadband becomes widely available, Internet conferencing will increasingly include live video images of all participants as they talk. Research how this works, and analyze its effect on group dynamics.

Using Your Whole Brain

Without planning it very much, engage a group of friends or classmates in a creative and enjoyable task, something out of the ordinary like a group art piece, an improv act, a group song writing, or a human sculpture. Join right in as part of the group. When you are finished, have a discussion about group members' feelings. Later, reflect on what happened in terms of concepts from this chapter.

THEORY TO ACTION

Get permission to observe several groups in action. These might be committees, boards, clubs, business meetings, or planning sessions. Do not participate; stay strictly in an observer role. Before your observation sessions, make a checklist of concepts from this chapter and analyze each group in terms of these points.

CASES

My Case: The Group Assignment*

Dr. Molto came into class with a huge box. "Let's test your group communication skills," he said. He divided the class into three groups and said, "Get comfortable; you'll need lots of space. Here's the assignment: You have the whole period, one hour and fifty minutes, to design and construct a model home. The only rule is that you can only use the materials I will give you. Next period, I want each group to show its model and discuss the group process." He then unloaded the box and passed out the blades, cards, pens, ice cream sticks, tape, glue, paper, and paper clips—an ample supply for each group.

Group One got right to work. They thought this would be fun, and everybody excitedly threw out ideas. Several people were talking at once, and no one seemed to take control. Molly spread the materials out on the floor in the middle of the group, and others started to grab different materials. Ben began building a little fence out of paper clips, and Bob constructed a mailbox from cards. Tom and Sally worked together to sketch a floor plan, while Molly laid sheets of paper together to make a roof. "Hey," she said, "I need walls." "Okay," Tom said as he finished his floor plan with Sally, and he stapled several cards together and handed them to Sally: "Here, cut some windows in this."

Group One laughed and shared what they had done. Then they put it together. The walls did not fit the roof, and although Sally cut a funny window in one wall with a razor blade, the house had no door. Bob's mailbox was twice the size of the house, and Tom and Sally's floor plan never did get used. Ben set up his paperclip fence in front of the house, or what appeared to be the front. They glanced at the clock. Forty-three minutes had gone by. "This was really fun," Sally said, as the group gathered up their things and left.

Group Two did not get into the exercise very well. They sat for a long time without saying much, although Sue and Shirley whispered quietly to one another about some private matter. In a few minutes Dr. Molto started to walk toward the group, and Jim said, "Well, I guess we need a design. What do you all think we should do?" No one answered. Jim then got out a piece of paper and drew up a hasty plan. "Here, Sue," he said. "You can tape four cards together to make the four walls, and Shirley, you can tape two cards together to make a roof. Okay?" Then he turned to Walter. "Um, Wanna make a tree?" "Okay," Walter said. "And, Jim, draw on some doors and windows with a magic marker." The house was done in about twelve minutes, and the group nervously got out books and started to study.

Group Three began somewhat haltingly. They weren't sure exactly what was expected, so they called the professor over to ask him what he wanted. "It's really entirely up to you," Dr. Molto said. After a few minutes, the group seemed to gain a little confidence and started generating ideas. There was a lot of disagreement at first about things like how elaborate the design should be, how big the model should be, and what kind of home design to create.

Shelby said, "Look, we have to get this done, so it can't be too elaborate, but we don't want something dumb either. I suggest that we make a fairly simple home, but include a few interesting features just to show some creativity." Without much debate, the group agreed, and they got to work. They shared ideas about basic design and dimensions and talked about how to use the materials. By the end of the first hour, the group was really excited about the idea and agreed openly that the model would be really cute. They divided up the construction labor, and Shelby took the role of making sure that each person's part fit into the design. They didn't quite finish by the end of the period, but Don volunteered to put on the finishing touches before the next period.

*(*A fictionalized account based on numerous experiences of the author in classroom group assignments.)*

My Analysis: These three groups had rather different experiences. They were all facing the same objective task characteristics, but their group-task characteristics and group structural characteristics were entirely different. Groups One and Two had serious problems, but Group Three seemed to achieve success both in the quality of the product and group satisfaction. It was probably the only group that had good effective synergy, or an assembly effect. Group One lacked task leadership, and Group Two lacked the stimulation that good social leadership can provide.

Group One had high individual productivity. Everybody was involved, but there was little coordination and consequently little group productivity. There was no conflict, and everybody seemed to have a great time. The interpersonal rewards were high, but the task rewards were not. The decision quality of Group One was not very good for several reasons. First, the group failed to properly assess what they were expected to do. They should have spent more time discussing the task and how to approach it. They had no goals and did not take the time to share information and ideas. The group's failures may have resulted from an unfortunately large number of dominant, friendly members.

Group Two had a clear task leader, but lacked stimulation. Only one member was productive and merely told the others what to do with little discussion. The resulting house was not very satisfying, and the group had no interpersonal satisfaction from the task. The group failed to discuss the positive and negative qualities of the original design, and no one was willing to come up with anything better. The group badly needed socioemotional leadership, especially in reintegration and tension reduction. There was a great need in this group for friendliness and dramatizing. The members tended to be unfriendly, negative, obedient, and passive.

Group Three created an excellent model home and enjoyed both task and interpersonal satisfactions in the process. They took time to figure out what they were doing, shared ideas, were not afraid to disagree, reached consensus, and made good use of both material and time resources. There seems to have been a strong task leader in the group, and socioemotional needs also seemed to get met. The group seemed to have a positive blend of interpersonal personalities. This group went through a clear progression of decision making from orientation, through conflict, to emergence and reinforcement.

Your Case and Analysis: Build a House

Get a group of friends or classmates together, gather some materials, and design and build a model home. After you are finished, analyze the group experience in terms of the concepts in this chapter.

CRITICAL INCIDENT

Go-Carts

You are a homeowner in a small housing development on the outskirts of your city. One Sunday morning while perusing the newspaper, you spot a small item that reads, 'Go-Cart Track Planned." The article only says that someone named Owen Garfield is planning to build a go-cart track on a lot adjacent to your housing development, just three blocks from your own house.

A go-cart track! No way. You can see it now (or rather hear it): constant noise, especially at night. Cars lining the street. Irresponsible kids coming and going all the time. It takes you about thirty seconds to realize that this is an inappropriate place for such a facility.

You immediately decide to approach some neighbors and try to stop the plan. You realize that this will take some doing and that the neighbors will need to meet and organize. You hope that someone else will take charge, but after mentioning it to several neighbors, all of whom share your alarm, no one comes forward to get things started. Time is wasting.

Okay. It's up to you. How will you proceed, and what do you need to do to mobilize the neighborhood successfully? How can Chapter 13 help you?

NOTES

Communication Theory and Scholarship

Theory in the Proce

System Theory

Theories of Signs a

Theories of Discou

Theories of Messag

Theories of Messag

Theories of Symbo

Theories of Social a

Theories of Experie

Critical Theories

Communication in

Communication in

Communication in Organizational Networks

Communication and Media

Chapter 14

Communication and Organizational Networks

- What is an organizational network?
- How can networks be understood in various ways?
- How does communication function to organize human relationships within a network?
- How are order, control, and coordination established within an organizational network?
- How does communication create organizational culture?

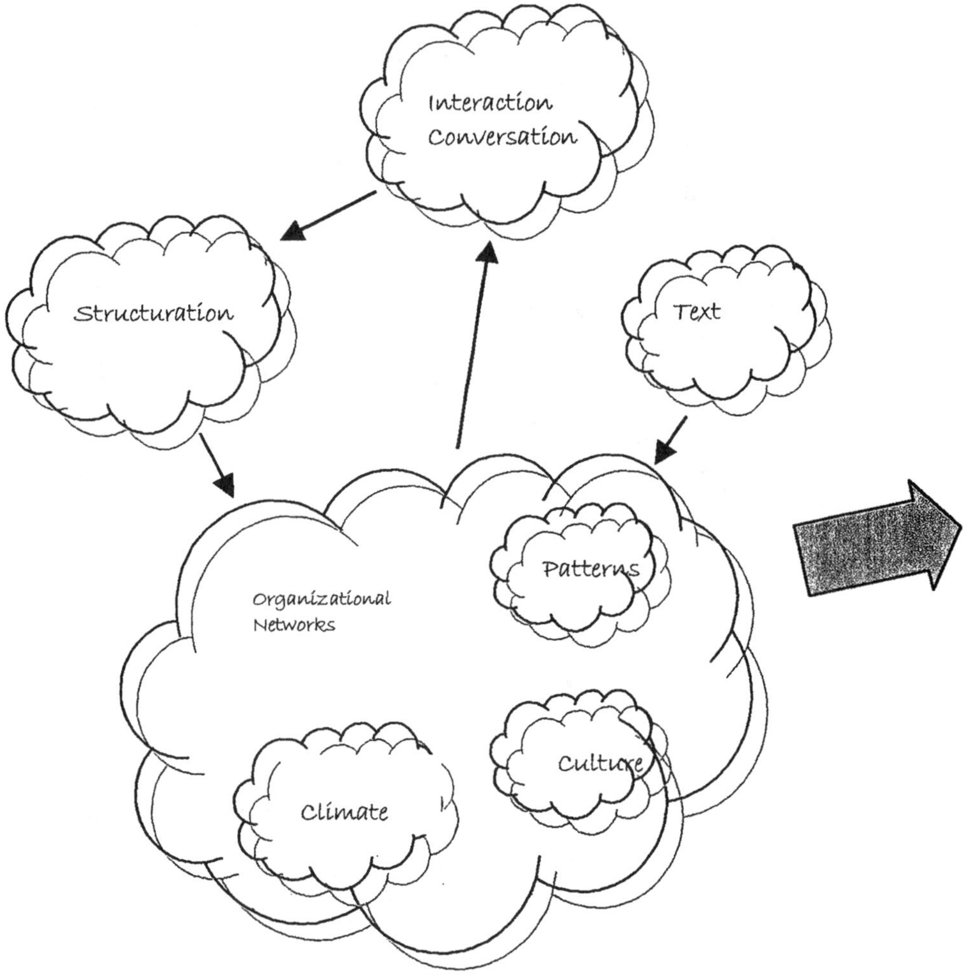

Chapter 14 Map
Communication and Organizational Networks

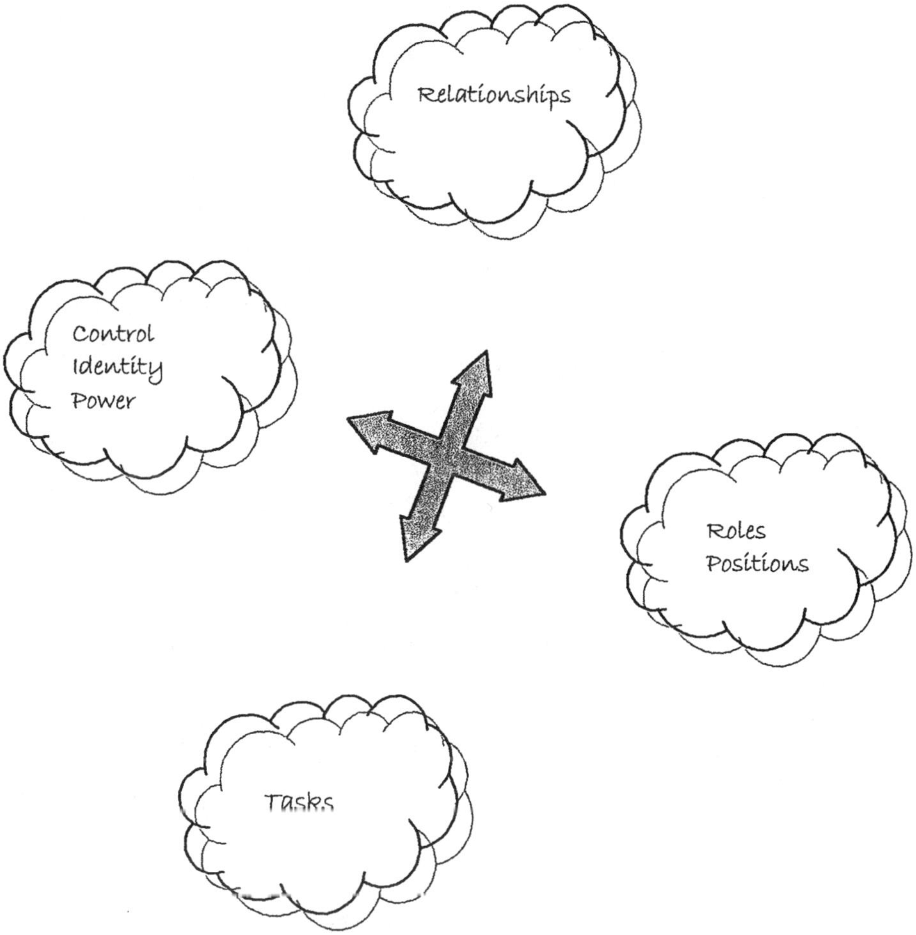

Make a Map
How would you map this chapter differently? Try it several ways and see what you learn.

WORD PUZZLE

Below is a list of terms and examples. Draw a line between each example and the term that best characterizes it.

Equivocality	Fred and Inez talk through a problem to clarify the situation.
Identification	Rafael is appointed as a go-between to coordinate information between the Manufacturing and Sales Departments.
Reception	Yoshi prepares an organizational chart for his work group.
Liaison	Over the years Carol has become close with many co-workers, and some of her best friends are the people she works with.
Participative Management	Ole shifts his lunch hour to 11:30 after management decides to implement a split-lunch policy.
Text	Judy leads a work team that makes all of its own decisions internally through discussion and consensus.

NOTES

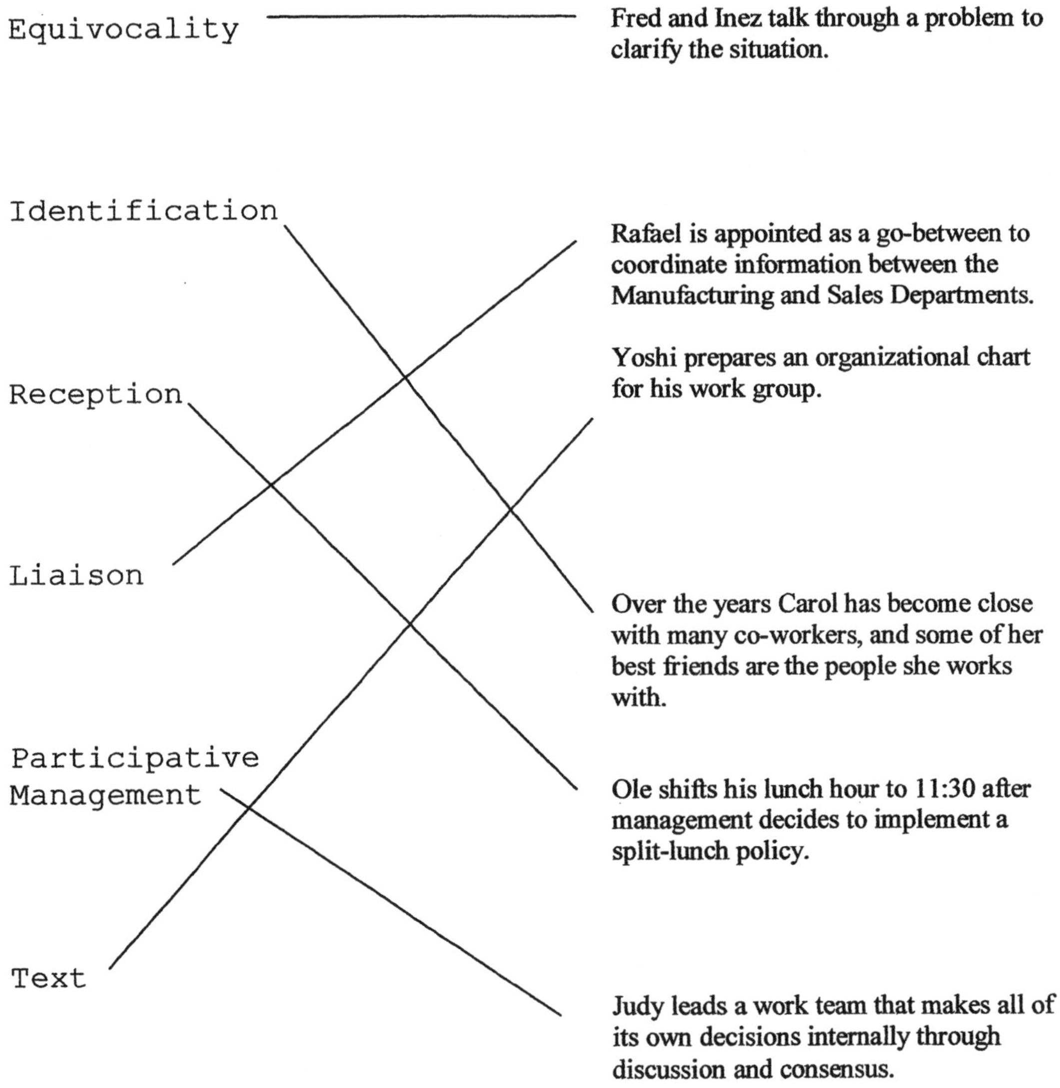
Equivocality
Identification
Reception
Liaison
Participative Management
Text
Fred and Inez talk through a problem to clarify the situation.
Rafael is appointed as a go-between to coordinate information between the Manufacturing and Sales Departments.
Yoshi prepares an organizational chart for his work group.
Over the years Carol has become close with many co-workers, and some of her best friends are the people she works with.
Ole shifts his lunch hour to 11:30 after management decides to implement a split-lunch policy.
Judy leads a work team that makes all of its own decisions internally through discussion and consensus.

CHALLENGES

Internet Challenges

Check out websites for at least one organization in each of the following categories. See what you can learn about the communication within these organizations. How do communication patterns vary from one category to another?

- Major corporation
- Small local firm
- Non-profit agency
- Governmental agency
- Youth group
- School or college
- Church or religious organization
- Support group or agency
- Club

Using Your Whole Brain

Design an ideal organization from scratch. Be creative and visionary. After you imagine this organization, go back and explain your choices in terms of the concepts from this chapter.

THEORY TO ACTION

Get permission to shadow a busy office worker in a service organization. Your job will be to stay with this person all day for one complete day, taking notes on what they are doing. Pay especially close attention to their communications—who, when, and how. Address the following questions:

1. What can you tell about this person's place in the network?
2. What network roles does this person take?
3. How does this person use communication to reduce uncertainty?
4. Notice how this person and others work things out in a process of co-orientation.
5. Would you say that this person acts primarily in a site of conception, implementation, or reception?
6. How would you characterize the organizational climate?
7. What forms of control is the person involved in?
8. How would you characterize the organizational culture?

CASES

My Case: Minfield County Transit*

One of the first things a person who is interested in public transit notices when arriving in Minfield County is that the buses are three different colors. Looking a little closer the person finds out that there are actually three separate routes, one operated by the Minfield Transit Authority (MTA), one operated by the City of Fixata Ravine (FRTS), and Hoover City's Transit Service (HCTS).

Fixata Ravine started bus service in 1975, followed by the Hoover City in 1976. While these two bus systems serve the citizens of their respective cities, MTA provides county-wide service including travel along the corridor that runs between the two cities.

The County service is co-owned and co-funded by both the Hoover City and Minfield County on the basis of about a 75/25 split with the majority of the money coming from the city. In contrast, FRTS is owned, funded, and operated solely by the City of Fixata Ravine. MTA is a Joint Powers Agency comprised of representatives from Minfield County and five northern and central area cities, including Hoover City and Fixata Ravine. The members entered into an agreement which spells out the percentage of total funding for which each member of the Joint Powers Agency is responsible.

As with most public transit systems, fare-box revenues in the area cover only about 20 - 30% of total costs. Thus, most of the funds that are used to support transit come from tax dollars. Because of this heavy subsidization the three service providers are required to prepare formal planning documents. The county is required to prepare, in addition, a comprehensive regional transportation plan. Finally, because of the complex funding and service relationships, a consulting firm was hired to prepare a regional transit study.

The transportation plan and the transit study both highlighted the existing problems with coordination between the three providers and noted that alternative designs for transit service should be developed and compared. The transit study stated that effective service planning was difficult because coordination of transit services was so fragmented and complex. The transit study went on to discuss the funding problems at length and noted that the county, which contributes a substantial share of the money, does not have a commensurate role to play in the management or administration of the services. What's more, while MTA plays a major role in guiding transit policy in the area, it has to rely entirely on others for its funding support.

The consultants came up with four alternative solutions: (1) development of cooperative service planning and monitoring efforts; (2) major modification to the Joint Powers Agreement for MTA; (3) consolidation of administration of the three providers; or (4) consolidation of operations and administration of the three. As a short-term improvement the consultants recommended the first alternative, and thus, a new entity, the Service Coordination Committee (SCC), was born. SCC is chaired by the executive director of a county coordinating agency which has its own board. All three of the service providers are members. Other members are representatives of the state department of transportation (a major source of funding) and of the local colleges (a major source of transit riders). This formally recognized committee replaced and expanded an existing informal committee. The main differences between the old and new committees were that formalities such as minutes were observed and that there was an implied threat of loss of funding should one of the three providers not participate and cooperate.

Although the consultants saw the implementation of alternative #1 as short-term solution and recommended escalation to alternative #2 for the longer term and even to alternative #3 should the first two alternatives not be, SCC was still attempting to function three years after the study was published. Members of SCC report that the widely divergent points of view among the providers that existed prior to the creation of SCC still exist. MTA's management comes from the old school, thinks that all the time spent in meetings is a waste, tends to ignore the process, and often does what it wants without notifying the others. FRTS's representative expects all changes to be discussed prior to implementation since that is the way it is done by Fixata Ravine's city government. The County representative often seems ambivalent due, no doubt, to being caught in a bind between a city that wants to have more control over the services its citizens receive and the reality of having to rely on MTA's operational expertise.

Some suggest that there was less candor between the members once minutes were being taken. Others note that there is little effective community participation—the representatives from the colleges rarely attend meetings, and there are no other community representatives. The chair of the SCC is very concerned not only about the climate within SCC, but also about its mission: making sure the citizens of Minfield County will get the best value for their tax-cum-transit dollar.

My Analysis: When viewed from the perspective of network theory, the overall transit system to the citizens of Minfield County can be seen as a suprasystem. Each of the transit providers—the county, the cities, and SCC—can each be considered a subsystem. The state and the local colleges are systems that are linked to the overall transit system via funding and riders.

Prior to the creation of the SCC there was an informal network for communication between the three providers: their informal operations committee. Once SCC was established this network was formalized and expanded. Now it includes the state, the colleges, and yet another county agency. The members of SCC who represent the transit providers can be seen as bridges, while the chair who is not affiliated with any of the three providers can be seen as a liaison. Although the whole idea behind creation of SCC seems to be the elimination of isolates, it appears that MTA management fills that network role in practice if not in theory.

SCC provides much needed centrality in that it is like a hub of all transit planning for the area. All of the providers have at least this one common activity and place to bring their issues. Although this network has few people in it, it is very dense and there seem to be at least two functions involved: funding and coordination of service. The participation of the state and college representatives provide interorganizational links.

Weber would be overjoyed to see how much bureaucracy has grown up around the provision of transit services in Minfield County. Power is tied to the funding which is why MTA participates even though its management thinks that such meetings are a waste of time. The degree to which this power is considered legitimate is somewhat more questionable. It is not clear that SCC actually has the authority to enforce any rules it may create. Yes, the members have to belong and say they are going to coordinate their activities, but for at least one of them this is only lip service, and there don't seem to be any consequences levied.

Perhaps there is too much overlap in the spheres of competence in this system. While Hoover City seems to have decided that MTA has better operational capabilities and has chosen to use them, that certainly is not the case for Fixata Ravine. What's more, there is no clear hierarchy here. The chair is not in place because of superior knowledge and training in the field of transit, but because a moderator is needed. With the state, the county, and every other agency in local government vying for the same funds, it is nearly impossible for these bureaucrats to allocate resources free of outside pressure. With all the reports and minutes in this system, the requirement for records seems to be being addressed. On second thought, perhaps Weber wouldn't be so happy after all. This bureaucracy doesn't work the way he said they should.

Certainly, Likert's System 4—the participative system—is the goal of such a system as has been set up here. Since there is no management which makes the final decision, all decisions must be participative. The problem seems to be that without at least one person to decide that everyone MUST play, some have decided not to. MTA goes its own way in an almost System-1 manner. They neither participate, consult, nor do they seem particularly benevolent when they go off and do things without even telling the others. It is not surprising that the FRTS's representative who is accustomed to a participative, System 4, environment would find this situation difficult.

It appears that there has been an effort to use concertative control in this system as well as bureaucratic control. It would appear that the dissident member, MTA, believes more in the use of simple control, however. The formal rules that have been established do not seem to be working because they have few teeth. Because MTA does not apparently feel related to the others in the system in any real way, it is unlikely that concertive control works in their case. Only when the loss of funding looms on the horizon do they get with the program.

There is no single overall organizational culture in this suprasystem. Even though the public who pays for the service and the riders who need the service need all of the parts of this system to work together efficiently and effectively, they do not. It doesn't seem likely that they will either. They do not share goals and they are all trying to get their hands on the same dollars. Just this competition alone could be enough to create a large wedge among them.

It appears that the way transit service is organized in Minfield County is not working very well. It is not clear what the real underlying organization is, but it is unlikely that it is what is appearing on any organizational charts. When the consultants said that the coordination was complex, they were right on. It appears that there are too many players and too much political pressure involved.

Whoever does have some legitimate power in this system—and it's not clear from the case who that is—will have to exert some leadership to identify the goals for transit service in Minfield County and establish incentives so that all the providers truly communicate and cooperate with each other. Once they are doing that there is a chance that they can begin the process of organizing in a way that will provide the level of service expected of them.

*Adapted from a case study by Robert Gray.

Your Case: The New Director*

Leo had been with Staraway Systems for two years as manager of the in-house communications program when Joyce, the director of his department, was made Vice President of International Affairs. Joyce had worked hard, built up a good reputation, and deserved the promotion. Leo was happy for her, but he wasn't sure what it would be like with a new boss.

Leo had done what he thought best with his program. Since the company had tripled in size to 10,000 employees in the two years he had been there, he now had a group of six people working with him. There were several other groups in the department and their managers, like Leo, had been handpicked by Joyce. Each had his or her own style, but they all flourished in the working environment Joyce had created.

Joyce called regular meetings of the managers in her department. They discussed their programs and kept each other informed. When they had a major project going that required the entire department's effort, they would sit down and go over all the issues and come to a consensus on how to attack the problem. Each of them was convinced that their high productivity was the result of the way they worked together.

Each of the managers who had worked for Joyce was given an opportunity to interview the candidates being considered as her replacement. Leo was favorably impressed by Matthew Cramer. This guy had worked with some of the big names in the industry and was able to discuss the technical issues with ease. Leo was concerned about Cramer's management style and the candidate answered in a straightforward manner. He definitely believed in participative management. Cramer got Leo's vote.

Not all of the managers in the department were as impressed with Cramer as Leo had been. One expressed reservations about not only Cramer's management style, but even went so far as to question his technical skills. Leo decided that it was probably just a mild case of sour grapes which would go away when Cramer came on board and the team got to know him.

Cramer arrived. It happened that just at that time there was a crisis which Leo felt Cramer could not be expected to know how to handle. Since some of the managers were not so supportive of Cramer, Leo decided to work harder and convinced his team to do lots of overtime to get the job done. It was a huge success, and Leo was overjoyed to see that Cramer gave Leo's employees much recognition for the fine job they had done. Leo and his staff all received very generous bonuses. Leo didn't notice until later, however, that his role in the effort had not been mentioned in the statements that Cramer had made publicly.

This was pointed out by the other managers, and Leo excused it as an oversight. Then one day Cramer called a staff meeting. He said there was going to be a massive reorganization, and they were going to have an off-site meeting to discuss it. A week later all the managers, Cramer, and a facilitator from Human Resources met at a local conference center. Cramer laid out why he thought the change was needed, and the discussion began. Some did not agree that there was any need for change; while not seeing the need for the change, others more or less accepted it and began offering suggestions about how to go about it. Only the two new managers who Cramer had brought in after he was hired seemed to find the reorganization to be imperative.

The group continued the discussion until lunch time, broke for lunch and returned early in the afternoon. A couple of the old-time managers had called some of the people in their groups to get their reactions to the new idea and to elicit suggestions from them. They shared this feedback with Cramer when the meeting reconvened. He smiled and nodded.

About an hour before the group broke for the day Cramer stood and began talking. He started by stating the date by which the reorganization would be complete. Hands flew up. How could the managers possibly get feedback from their staffs to him in so short a time? He made calming motions with his hands and told them that of course their staff members would be kept informed. More similar questions were followed by just about the same answers. When the managers left they weren't sure what they had heard and what was happening.

Two weeks later Cramer held a departmental meeting to which attendance was mandatory. He announced the reorganization. Leo and the other managers just looked at each other when Cramer referred to the off-site meeting as if all this had been agreed upon there. Leo went back to his work area and began the task of calming his staff.

Cramer started calling every-morning meetings at 8:00 AM to discuss the events of the previous day. Now this was relevant to Joe whose job was security, but not to the rest of the managers, but they ALL had to be there. Leo found himself working sixteen and twenty hour days.

When Cramer had been there two months, the manager who had been very skeptical of him was demoted. One of Leo's best employees was asked to take over the area to help out. Later, however, when the job was to be filled permanently, Theo was told he didn't qualify for the position. This didn't make sense to Theo or Leo since Theo had a Master's degree and seven years of management experience prior to coming to Staraway. It appeared that once again, Cramer had a friend he thought better suited to the job. Theo quit.

Cramer convinced top management of the firm that a new $2 million computer system was needed for the company. Without consulting the people in his department who would have to do the work, he committed to having the system operational in less than 18 months. Leo felt this date was impossible to make given the scope of the project and went to talk to Cramer. He suggested that the date be moved. Cramer said, "No, that's the date top management expects." Leo then suggested doing part of the project by that date, but phasing in the rest. Again, the answer was no. Leo left the department. The project ended up being $1 million over budget and 12 months late.

Your Analysis: Using the concepts in Chapters 12-14 describe what is going on here. Discuss it from the standpoint of three or more of the theorists you have studied.

*Adapted from a case study by Roberta Gray.

CRITICAL INCIDENT

The Academy

You are on the faculty of Johns Academy, a well-known local and regional private institution. Johns is a military school covering grades 7-12, and the student body consists of 700 cadets. The Academy, now in its ninetieth year, began admitting girls about 12 years ago, and the ratio is now about two-thirds boys and one-third girls. The school has a long history of success, always has twice as many applicants as spaces available, draws considerable tuition, has a rock-solid endowment, and sends over 80% of its graduates on to college. A respectable number of graduates go on to major military academies and ROTC, and many of these end up in military careers.

Recently you became Dean of Students. In your first meeting with the President, he confirmed what you already knew, that students seem to be losing their discipline and commitment. Dress standards have been dropping, tardiness and absenteeism are up, and there seems to be a general laxness. The President asks you to make this problem a priority and to try to turn things around.

Develop a plan for attacking this problem, using Chapter 14 as a guide.

Chapter 15

Communication and Media

- How do media influence culture?
- How do media respond to and affect audiences?
- How do media function as a social institution?
- What are the effects of media depictions?
- How do people use media?

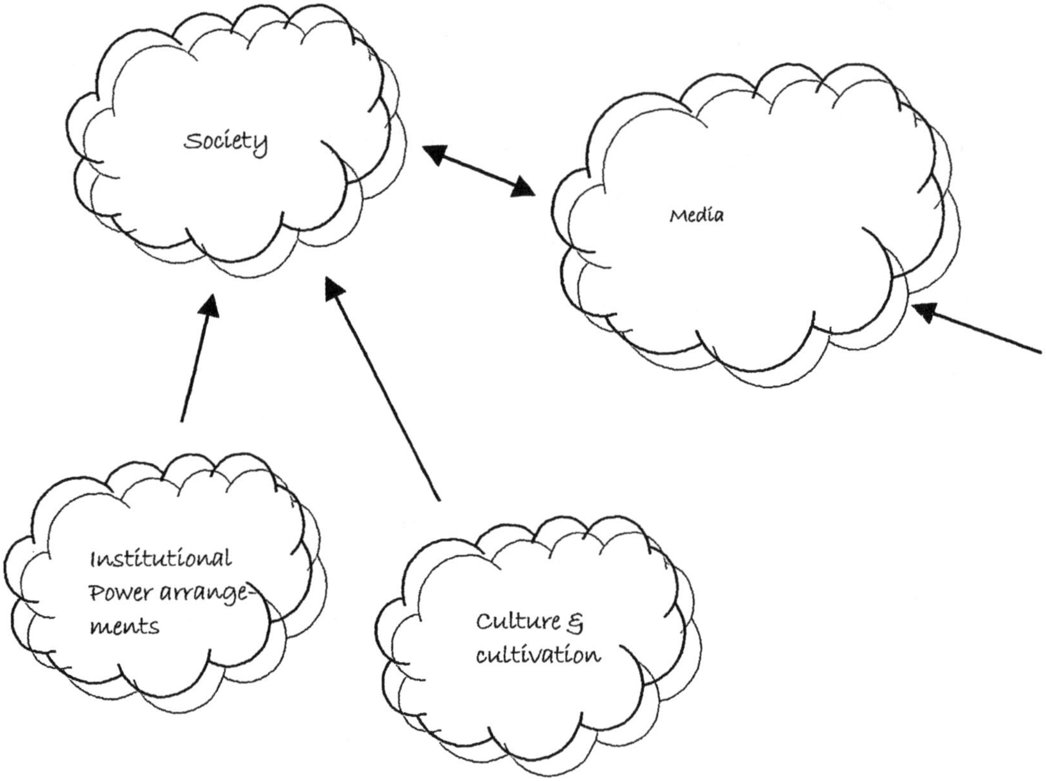

Chapter 15 Map
Communication and Media

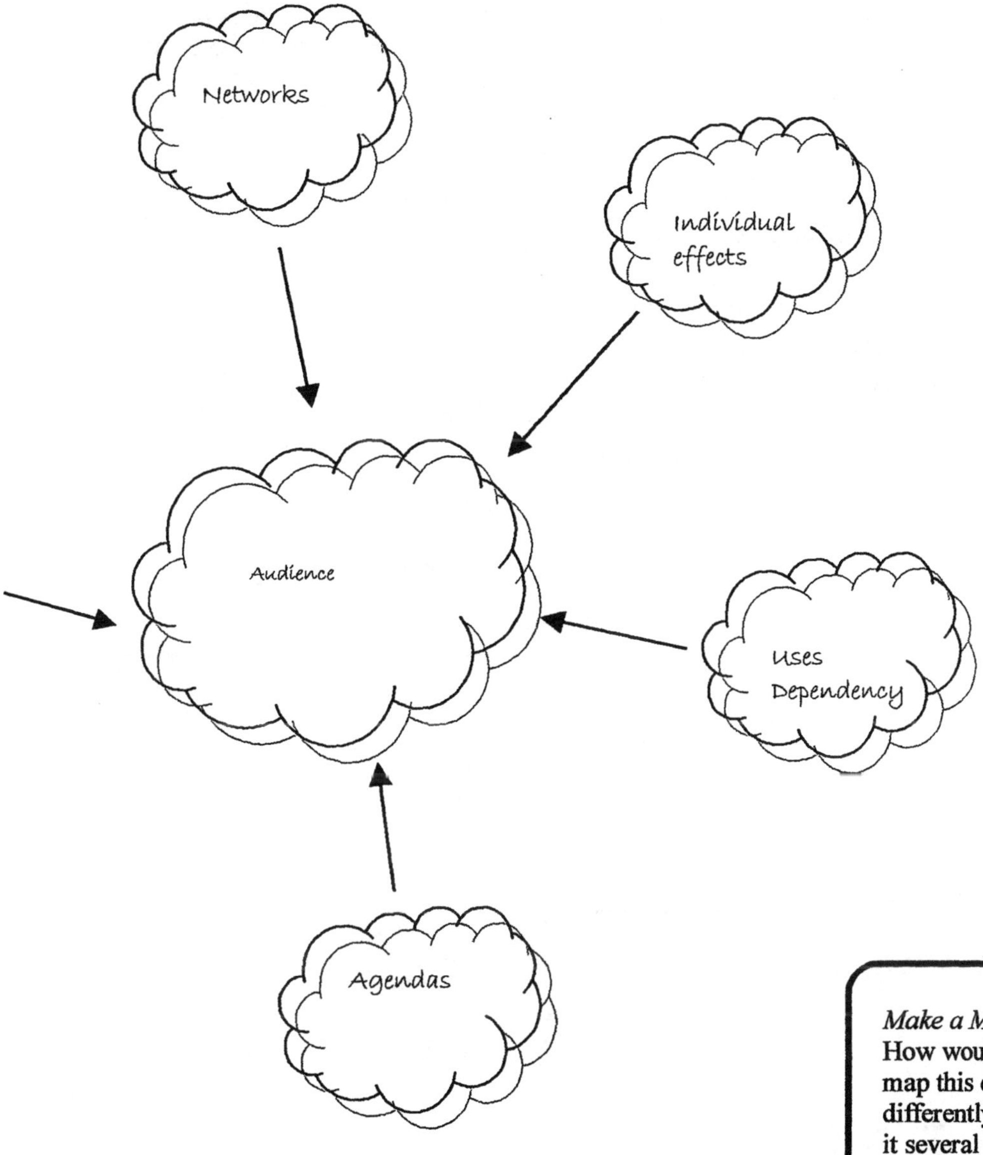

Make a Map
How would you map this chapter differently? Try it several ways and see what you learn.

WORD PUZZLE

Below is a numbered list of terms from the chapter. Under these are a set of clues. Each clue corresponds to another term from the chapter. Determine each unknown term by using the clue. Each letter of the new term must also appear in the numbered term indicated under the space for that letter.

1. Jean Baudrillard
2. Sociocultural approach
3. Hegemonic theory
4. Two-step flow hypothesis
5. Monomorphism
6. Pseudoenvironment
7. Expectancy-value theory
8. Interactive communication

Clues:	*Terms:*
Producer's content	___ ___ ___ ___ ___ ___ ___ ___ 1 5 7 2 6 4 8 3
______ of silence	___ ___ ___ ___ ___ ___ 2 6 3 2 1 7
Salient issues	___ ___ ___ ___ ___ ___ 2 3 6 7 1 2
Outcome	___ ___ ___ ___ ___ ___ 7 4 4 6 8 3
Inspiration of many critical theorists	___ ___ ___ ___ 5 1 8 7
Being scapegoated	___ ___ ___ ___ ___ ___ ___ 6 1 2 1 2 8 4

NOTES

Answers:

Producer's content	E N C O D I N G
______ of silence	S P I R A L
Salient issues	A G E N D A
Outcome	E F F E C T
Inspiration of many critical theorists	M A R X
Being scapegoated	P I L L O R Y

CHALLENGES

Internet Challenges

Much media programming is now available on the Internet. In a search, find as many interfaces as you can between mass media and the Internet. Check out news, entertainment, music, video, radio, magazines, and any other outlets you can think of. Spend a little time with some of these sites, and answer the following questions:

1. How is the Internet as a medium different from traditional mass media? How is it the same?
2. Does medium theory apply to the Internet? Why or why not?
3. How do audiences use media content differently when it is delivered on the Internet?
4. How might the outcomes and effects of Internet media be different from traditional forms of media.

Now think ahead 50 years. Take the role of futurist and imagine what the Internet, or whatever form has evolved by then, will look like. How do you think the relationship between the traditional media and the "Internet" will be different then? How will traditional media have changed by then?

Using Your Whole Brain

What is your favorite medium? What do you most like about it? How does it capture your imagination and attention? Go there now. Turn on your favorite television program, listen to the radio, pick up the newspaper, grab some comic books, or whatever you like to do in your media world. Just take this in for a few minutes, keeping in touch with your feelings and reactions. How would you characterize your interaction with this medium from a right-brain point of view? Now go back to the chapter and see what concepts resonate with your intuitive experience.

THEORY TO ACTION

Conduct a media critique session with a group of friends, associates, or classmates. Spend at least one hour looking critically at the role, influences, and place of media in our society. What problems do you discover? After the session think seriously about the role of media in your own life. What changes would you like to make in your relationship to media? How would you go about making these changes? Plan a course of action.

CASES

My Case: The Visitors*

Last summer Joe, Susan, and their two-year-old son, Chris came to visit. Our family consists of a mother, father, and two boys ages eight and twelve. The twelve-year-old's idea of great entertainment is MTV which he sees mostly at his friends' houses. The eight-year-old likes anything that doesn't have "mushy stuff" in it. Joe and Susan brought three videocassettes full of "Sesame Street" programs for Chris.

Chris is a very active child, and his parents use the "Sesame Street" tapes to keep him occupied when they are busy at home. They monitor what he watches carefully, and that is why they bring the tapes along with them, just in case there is nothing suitable for him on TV. While we were eating breakfast on Saturday morning Chris got very impatient so his parents allowed him to leave the table and turned on one of the tapes they had brought. This was at about 9:00 A M.

Four hours later Chris, Joe, and our two boys were still staring at "Sesame Street." Had I told our boys that they had to watch four hours of "Sesame Street" they would have let me know they weren't babies and that was kid stuff, but there they were—almost hypnotized. After finally getting everyone away from the TV we went on with our day, and I announced that we would NOT have "Sesame Street" on the next morning. Joe, Susan and Chris left early on Sunday.

My Analysis: This is a small episode in the media life of a family. The fact that this—and presumably many other episodes—revolved around the television is testimony to the importance of media in our lives. Specifically, Sesame Street is an important socializing agent for many children. It certainly cultivates a common culture among the millions of children who view it regularly, and many critical theorists would point out that dominant interests in our society are promoted by the preferred reading of this program. The problem with this kind of hegemony is that children usually do not have the intelligence to create oppositional readings, and many parents do not have the motivation to do so.

In this episode the program probably fulfilled primarily an entertainment function for the children, a function the parents readily accepted because it allowed them time away from the demands that the children might otherwise have made on their time and attention. The story does show how our media habits are situated in a small group context, in this case the family. This Saturday morning's viewing was not an isolated event, but was connected to other aspects of the family system. The viewing began when Chris's parents encouraged him to watch the tapes because he was apparently disturbing the adult's breakfast-table talk. Later the reporter began to feel uncomfortable about the amount of viewing the children were doing and decided not to allow them to watch television the following morning. Here we see that family rituals, norms, and values affect how people use media. Thus, this story refutes the idea of the mass society audience.

Perhaps the most useful theories for understanding the events of this case are uses and gratifications and dependency theory. Clearly, both the parents and the children have come to rely on certain television programming to meet particular needs and in the process have become dependent upon them. We do not have enough information to tell what the effects of this dependency may be, but we can be fairly confident that the dependency patterns have become established.

*Adapted from a case study by Roberta Gray.

Your Case: A Media Self-Analysis

Write a personal media uses, gratifications, and dependency analysis. What media do you depend on and why? How do you use media to meet various needs? Illustrate Figure 15.5 from the text with two or three examples from your own life.

CRITICAL INCIDENT

Watching T.V.

You are the parent of a one-year-old son. You notice lately that your boy is orienting more and more toward the television set. You realize that you must decide soon what kind of policy to have regarding your child's television viewing. You want to start early before viewing habits become established.

How will you deal with your child's television viewing? How can Chapter 15 help you establish a family television policy?

NOTES